Focaccia

CAROL FIELD

Focaccia

simple breads from the italian oven

photographs by joyce oudkerk pool

CHRONICLE BOOKS

SAN FRANCISCO

Library of Congress Cataloging-in-Publication Data available.

ISBN 0-8118-4065-4

Manufactured in China.

Book and cover design by Aufuldish & Warinner
Cover photograph prop styling by Tabletop Prop
Cover photograph food styling by Pouké

Distributed in Canada by Raincoast Books
9050 Shaughnessy Street
Vancouver, British Columbia V6P 6E5

10 9 8 7 6 5 4 3 2 1

Chronicle Books LLC
85 Second Street
San Francisco, California 94105

www.chroniclebooks.com

Dedication

This book is for Gianna and Riccardo Bertelli,
friends from the very beginning of the Italian adventure.

Acknowledgments

❧

This book would not have been possible without the help of Italians and Americans alike. I am particularly grateful to Professore Luigi Sada, Paolo Lingua, Sonia Lorenzini and her mother Vittoria Lorenzini, Carlo Sarti, the Binelli family at Pizzeria Marconi in Forte dei Marmi, Alberto Scicchitano, Paolo Lillo, Carlo Sozzo, and the Guerra family at the Hotel Melograno in Monopoli. ❧ Daniela Falini, my wonderful researcher in Italy, helped me magnificently, as she always does. Faith Willinger was, as always, a source of knowledge, inspiration, and a fabulous travel companion. Special thanks to Arlene Wanderman and the International Olive Oil Council. Mary Risley found my two main testers, who were fabulous; major thanks to Pat Benson and Chris Engle. Other testers include Pat Adler, Cynthia Wardell, Gretchen Grant, and Linda Hughes. ❧ I owe very special thanks to Matthew who helped me through the complexities of the computer and miraculously made many files and chapters merge into a single book. ❧ Everyone at Chronicle Books has made this process remarkably pleasant; Leslie Jonath and Bill LeBlond have been extraordinary editors, Carolyn Miller a splendid copy editor and Susan Derecskey a wonderful proofreader. Fred Hill, as always, has been a wonderful agent. ❧ Once again, my wonderful husband John has survived yet another impassioned plunge into Italian food. And once again, Matthew and Alison have been enthusiastic and wonderfully supportive.

TABLE OF CONTENTS

Introduction 14

Making Perfect Focaccia 18

Four Basic Focaccia Doughs and One Starter 30

Savory Focaccia 38

Filled and Double-Layered Focaccia   80

Fillings for Focacce and Focaccine   90

Sweet Focaccia 98

INTRODUCTION

I S THIS THE BEGINNING OF THE GOLDEN AGE of focaccia? Will people who vividly recall their first encounter with pizza now look back nostalgically, remembering their initial bite into this delicious flat bread whose surface is fragrant with olive oil, crystals of sea salt, and the aromatic herbs that flourish on country hillsides? Pizza, its famous southern Italian cousin, may be America's favorite food, but focaccia is taking the country by quiet storm. Made of the simplest bread dough, to which olive oil is usually added, this delicious specialty may be rectangular or round, thin and crunchy or high and soft, crisp or chewy; it may be seasoned with a wash of tomatoes and a handful of capers, or ooze with cheeses, be carpeted with olives, or dappled with newly picked tomatoes, glossy ribbons of sweet pepper, or tangles of caramelized onions. In Italy, where focaccia has been made for millenia, bakers slide giant pans of the deeply fingerprinted dough into their high-fired ovens, pull them out again, and let them cool before cutting them into wedges or squares. *Focacce* may be sliced open and filled with cheeses and prosciutto and with fillings whose tastes are limited only by the cook's imagination. No matter how they are topped or filled, however, they are never served sizzling hot like a pizza.

FOCACCIA STARTS WITH A VERSATILE AND SIMPLE DOUGH THAT IS MUCH EASIER TO MAKE than most bread dough. It isn't formed into complicated shapes, and it is easy to handle. Just place it in an oiled baking pan, press the dough out to the edges, dimple it with your fingertips, flavor it with the fragrant ingredients of your choice, let it rise a bit, and bake it. This flat bread is sometimes shaped into small *focacce,* or *focaccine,* little discs made just to fit into the palm of the hand. That shouldn't come as a surprise, since these little breads were originally baked as a simple treat for children, hungry bystanders, and for the bakers themselves on the one day of the week that country women produced the family's bread. Eaten warm or at room temperature, focaccia can be a one-dish meal, a snack, or food for a picnic or a light meal. It can be served for breakfast, lunch, or dinner in place of bread, and may appear at all moments in between. It can be cut in half and filled with prosciutto and cheese or with all manner of spreads, and then be put in the oven to be heated. Focaccia is perfect for making sandwiches or for serving in small bites as part of an antipasto.

No one knows who invented the first focaccia, but the contribution, like the discovery of fire or creation of the wheel, has enriched the experience of the civilization that followed. In the beginning, grain was beaten with water into a batter that was cooked on heated stones. Focaccia once meant "an unleavened piece of flat bread"; the name comes from *focus,* the Latin word for fire, and the adjective *focacius* thus means "cooked with fire." By Roman times, guilds of bakers prepared breads using leavening, flour, water, and a fat such as olive oil, as well as various other ingredients to give the breads more flavor. They baked cheese focaccia on a bed of bay leaves much as the Italians in the Lunigiana region still set their *focacce* on chestnut leaves. The Romans offered some *focacce* as sacrifices to the gods and made others to sustain a hungry population.

Just as the Ur-pizza comes from Naples, the most famous focaccia comes from Genoa in Liguria, the region that stretches in a thin arc from the French border to the northern edge of Tuscany. The steep hillsides of its landscape are densely planted with the silvery green olive trees that produce the light fruity oil that flavors the focaccia. By the thirteenth century the ancient maritime republic of Genoa had filled its granaries with wheat, the great cash crop of the time, creating an economy and a cuisine based on the monopoly of grain. Then, as now, the Genoese ate their pasta and focaccia topped with glorious combinations of the herbs and vegetables that flourish in the soil.

Focaccia appears on Ligurian tables at least twice a day because it is the true bread of the region, although its flavorings change by zones and microclimates. The focaccia of Savoia is named *focaccia all'Andrea,* while in nearby San Remo it becomes *sardenaira,* where it includes *machetto,* a kind of anchovy or sardine paste made by local fishermen. Focaccia was once the specialty of the Genoa-Ventimiglia railroad line, where cries of *"focaccia, focaccia,"* echoed in the train station. During stops, boys in white jackets with baskets hanging from their arms proffered wax paper–wrapped triangles that were quickly snapped up by hungry commuters.

THERE ARE TWO DISTINCT TYPES OF SAVORY FOCACCIA IN ITALY: LOW CHEWY ONES THAT rise about ½ to ¾ inch, and much thicker ones from Puglia that get their height and soft texture from the presence of mashed potatoes in the dough. Savory focaccia, in particular, appears in every seafaring region. In earlier times outstanding bread was more easily made in the interior where the air is still and dry and the water soft, while those regions on the sea produced either focaccia, a primal flat bread, or its close relative, pizza. Ligurians are famous for their focaccia, which in Tuscany and Umbria is called *schiacciata* or *stiacciata* or *ciaccia* in dialect (all of which simply mean "flattened"). Venetians produce *fugassa,* which means "cooked under the ashes." The people of Puglia, with their legendary tradition of breads, make phenomenal focaccia and *schiacciata,* as do the Sicilians, who have given their flat breads myriad names that weave their way along the convoluted path between pizza and focaccia. One of Palermo's most famous dishes is focaccia topped with beef spleen that has been cooked in giant copper cauldrons.

KNOWING A GOOD THING WHEN THEY ATE IT, ITALIANS ALSO INVENTED SUGAR-SPIKED *focacce* to please their famous collective sweet tooth. Regional differences are clear: Tuscans took advantage of the grapes harvested in Chianti and tossed handfuls of Sangiovese grapes right into sweetened bread dough. They flavored their doughs with anise-scented elderberry flowers, with figs, and with walnuts, while people in the Milanese countryside carpeted their *focacce* with raisins and the Bolognese split theirs and filled them with ice cream.

I HAVE WANDERED ACROSS THE REGIONS OF ITALY SAMPLING FOCACCIA, DASHING INTO bakeries and settling into family homes to learn the secrets of how they are made. My delighted discovery is that this fragrant rustic bread is simple to make and every bit as versatile as pizza. It is meant to be eaten at any hour of the day, and its flavors satisfy in their simplicity, for they come from the best that nature has to offer. Start with a simple dough made of flour, water, yeast, and salt, flavor it with herbs, top it with fresh vegetables, drizzlings of olive oil, and crystals of salt that come from the sea, and you have a meal for any time. LET THE BAKING BEGIN!

MAKING PERFECT FOCACCIA

Ingredients

❀

Focaccia begins with the most basic of ingredients—flour, water, yeast, salt, sometimes a little olive oil—but it is much simpler to make than most other breads if you pay attention to a few uncomplicated rules.

YEAST Yeast is a living organism held in suspension that, once fed with warm water and flour, will awaken from its long sleep and begin to feed on the sugars present in the flour. You can buy it in $1/4$-ounce packets holding tiny fawn-colored granules of active dry yeast, or in $1/2$-ounce cakes of creamy fresh yeast. A package of active dry yeast measures about $2 1/2$ teaspoons and is equal to a cube of fresh yeast. If you plan to bake often, I suggest that you buy active dry yeast in bulk; it is made without preservatives and costs so much less that your savings will be immense.

❧ I do all my baking with active dry yeast because it keeps for months in the refrigerator or freezer, while fresh cake yeast is much more perishable—it has a life of about one week—and must be kept carefully wrapped and refrigerated. Active dry yeast is dissolved in warm water that is 105° to 115°F, while fresh yeast uses slightly cooler water (95° to 105°F). If you have any question about the liveliness of your yeast, first check the expiration date on the package, then whisk a little yeast and a pinch of sugar together in 1 cup of warm water (see above) and watch to see if it foams and bubbles within 10 minutes. If it doesn't, discard the yeast and buy a new supply.

❧ I do not recommend using rapid-rise yeasts. In speeding up the rising process, they rob the grain of the opportunity to develop its flavor. If you are concerned about time and want to fit making focaccia into the rhythms of your life, do as I do and opt for long, slow, cool rises. Yeasts do not die at cool temperatures; they simply work more slowly. I recommend cutting the yeast in a recipe to $1/2$ to $3/4$ teaspoon, making the dough in the evening, then placing it in the refrigerator to rise slowly overnight, or making it in the morning and leaving it all day in the refrigerator to rise and ripen slowly. When you are ready, take it out of the refrigerator, let it return to room temperature for about 2 hours, and proceed with the recipe.

FLOUR I learned from baking with Italian bread bakers and focaccia makers that they admire American flours extravagantly and would give anything to have a constant supply of them. Instead, they have to make do with weaker Italian flours, which they mix with our flour made from hard winter wheat in a 5 to 1 ratio, in order to give strength to their doughs.

❧ Almost all the *focacce* in this book are made with unbleached all-purpose flour, a delicate creamy-colored mixture of soft and hard wheats. Wheat flour contains a protein called gluten, whose elasticity allows the dough to expand when the once-dormant yeast has been mixed with water. As the yeast begins to eat the sugars in the flour, it creates bubbles of carbon dioxide that become enmeshed in the elastic gluten network and cause the dough to rise. If you look on the side of most bags of flour, you will find the gluten content listed as the quantity of protein. In most unbleached all-purpose flours, gluten ranges from 11 to 13 percent. When you are looking for flour, unbleached is the crucial word. It is sold at most groceries and supermarkets; Gold Medal, Pillsbury, Hecker's, and King Arthur are all well-distributed brands. Do not confuse it with bleached all-purpose flour, which is softer and has a gluten content ranging from 8 to 10 percent, although even that varies substantially from region to region. Similarly, do not substitute bread flour for unbleached all-purpose flour. Bread flour has a higher gluten content, absorbs more water, and needs a longer mixing time. It may also produce a tougher texture, but at any rate it will certainly produce a different product than these recipes intend.

❧ Organic stone-ground unbleached flours can add an exceptional flavor to focaccia. I would recommend them, especially for any focaccia made with a starter (such as Focaccia with Olive Oil and White Wine, page 66; or Schiacciata with Slivers of Potatoes and Rosemary, page 68), whose flavor depends heavily on the flavor of the wheat.

❧ Although these recipes were written and tested with precise amounts of flour, variations in flours and weather may produce different results. Stone-ground organic flours may absorb water differently than flours sold in the supermarket. Varying weather conditions and ambient temperatures can alter the proportions. If it is hot and humid, the flour will absorb moisture, while dry days may produce dry doughs that will need extra water, added a little bit at a time, until your dough matches the consistency and texture described in the recipe. To be absolutely safe, you may want to hold back about 1/2 cup of the flour when you begin the mixing process.

OTHER FLOURS There are two forms of whole-wheat flour used in these recipes. The smooth, fine-textured stone-ground whole wheat is the grind you are most likely to find in the grocery store. The coarser variety of whole wheat, which is sometimes labeled as graham flour, is ground from the entire hard red spring-wheat berry: husk, vitamin-rich wheat germ, and all. It feels gritty and, when you look closely, you can actually see large flecks of the bran. The coarser grind makes a much sturdier, chewier focaccia.

❧ Durum flour is a silky-textured golden flour milled from durum wheat, a hard, high-gluten strain of wheat that is an entirely different strain from the wheat normally used for making bread and focaccia. In its coarser, more granular form it is semolina flour, the same golden grain Italians use for making pasta. Be careful not to use either semolina or whole-wheat durum (*durum integrale* in Italian), which will not work in these recipes. Use durum by itself or in combination with unbleached all-purpose or spelt or *farro* flours. Semolina can be used like cornmeal to sprinkle on baking stones to prevent dough from sticking.

❧ White whole-wheat flour is a new strain of hard winter wheat that has recently been developed in America. It has the nutritional value of whole wheat, but has been bred without any of the compounds in the bran that give whole wheat its slightly bitter edge. When baked, this flour looks like a cross between white and whole wheat and has a sweet nutty flavor.

❧ Spelt is a primitive strain of wheat reminiscent in taste of one that was widely used by the ancient Romans and still appears in a few Italian regions such as Tuscany and Puglia. One variety of the grain is now being discovered in America, where it is valued not only for its taste but because it is a high-gluten wheat that some people who are normally allergic to other wheat can tolerate. Spelt flour produces a focaccia with a chewy texture and nutty flavor that make it especially attractive. There are both white and whole-wheat spelt flours. Because spelt flour absorbs moisture easily, recipes using it require less water than those made with unbleached all-purpose flour.

❧ Corn flour is a finely ground version of polenta or cornmeal. It can be stone-ground to produce a slightly gritty texture or water-ground for a silkier feel. Cornmeal has no gluten, so it must be combined with a substantial amount of wheat flour to make a dough that will rise. It gives taste and texture to focaccia doughs, and it may also be sprinkled on baking stones to keep doughs from sticking.

WATER If your water is treated with chemicals that have a noticeable flavor, you might want to use spring water. Don't buy distilled water, and please don't create any extra expense by opting for elegant imported bottled waters.

SALT Since focaccia is the product of Mediterranean countries, I follow local practice and use fine sea salt in the dough and coarse sea salt on top of the most straightforward varieties. Sea salt is the purest of all salts because it is the product of the slow evaporation of sea water. Rock salt and kosher salt are less salty-tasting than sea salt, while the commercial plain and iodized varieties are saltier in taste.

OLIVE OIL Focaccia couldn't exist without olive oil. Olive oil often flavors the interior of the dough, giving it suppleness and moisture, and it pools on top in the little holes created by dimpling the dough with your fingertips or knuckles. I brush oil over the edges of the dough immediately after taking it out of the oven to give it an added bit of moisture and shininess. Be sure to brush olive oil over each layer of dough in a filled focaccia. For an extra-crispy focaccia, spread 2 to 2 $\frac{1}{2}$ tablespoons of olive oil in the bottom of a large rectangular baking pan before stretching the dough to cover the bottom. Once it is baked, you can blot the focaccia on paper towels before setting it on a rack to cool.

❧ If I were being absolutely authentic, I would use light Ligurian extra-virgin olive oils when making focaccia from Liguria and switch to a somewhat heavier and fruitier oil when flavoring *focacce* from Puglia. Tuscans use Tuscan oils and Sicilians use Sicilians oils for their *focacce,* but for Americans that way lies madness, to say nothing of extravagance. All extra-virgin olive oils are made from the finest quality olives that are cold-pressed by a method that uses no extraction or heat. I recommend using a good extra-virgin olive oil, but not one of the very fruity or extremely expensive ones. The oil should give a delicate flavor and richness to the dough. "Pure" olive oil means merely that the oil is made solely of olives. I use pure olive oil for brushing all baking equipment, including perforated pizza pans.

Equipment

Since focaccia was probably one of the first breads ever baked in the world, making it should be very simple. If I had my way, I'd be certain that every baker had a very few pieces of extremely helpful equipment:

❧ A *scale* may not be the answer to making flawless focaccia, but it is an immense help. Everyone measures flour differently. Some people scoop flour from a densely packed bag just off the grocery shelf, while others pour the flour into a big mixing bowl and aerate it before scooping. The difference in measurements for a single recipe can be as much $\frac{1}{2}$ cup, a discrepancy sure to produce very different doughs. The only way to be certain that you are measuring correctly is to weigh your flour, so if it is at all possible, please use a scale. Otherwise, pour your flour into a container where it isn't tightly packed, scoop a cup into it, and level it off with a knife.

❧ A heavy-duty standing *electric mixer* is not a necessity because most of these doughs can be made by hand, but it makes mixing and kneading much easier. A heavy-duty mixer can handle wet doughs that are too moist and sticky to knead by hand. Be sure to mix with the paddle attachment and to switch to the dough hook for kneading. Do not use a lightweight mixer, because the motor may overheat.

❧ A *dough scraper, dough knife,* or *baker's bench knife* are all the same thing: a baker's best friend. This simple tool is a rectangular piece of stainless steel with a wooden or rolled stainless steel handle and a sharp edge. I couldn't live without it, since it does everything from handling sticky doughs at the beginning of the kneading process and dividing doughs, to moving them from one place to another and cleaning and scraping up bits of hardened dough that stick to the work surface.

❧ *Baking stones, unglazed quarry tiles,* or *$1\frac{1}{2}$-inch-thick refractory bricks* are the best way to replicate the interior of a baker's brick oven and make crunchy focaccia. They help draw moisture from the surface of the dough, they distribute heat evenly, and they retain the intense heat that makes crispy crusts. I prefer a single stone to several smaller tiles and advise you to buy the largest one you can find, preferably a rectangular one. I leave mine in the oven all the time, for cooking and baking everything but cookies and pastries. Set the baking rack on the lower or middle shelf and place the stone directly on it, leaving a 1-inch border so that air can circulate freely around it. No matter which method you use, place the stone in the oven and preheat to 425°F for at least 30 minutes before baking. If you want to clean the stone, tiles, or bricks, cool them completely first. You can wash them with cold water but never use soap, since its flavor would be absorbed by the porous material.

❧ *Pie pans* for baking focaccia come in 8-, 9-, or 10-inch rounds. The dark carbon steel, heavy aluminum, or anodized nonstick coated ones work best. For rectangular focaccia, use low-sided $10\frac{1}{2}$ x $15\frac{1}{2}$-inch jelly roll pans or 11 x 17-inch rimmed baking sheets or pans, preferably of a nonstick material.

A *work surface* for mixing and kneading focaccia should be at least 2 feet square and be high enough that you can mix and knead comfortably with your back straight and your hands extended. I prefer the warmth of a wood countertop, but good focaccia can be made on marble or granite or Formica, as long as it is easy to scrape clean after making each batch of dough.

A *wooden spoon* is perfect for mixing dough.

These are nice to have:

Parchment paper, or *baking parchment*, lines baking pans and baker's peels, making several of these moist and delicate doughs much easier to work with. Parchment paper can be cut to fit a baking pan or can be laid directly on a baking stone as long as it is trimmed so it doesn't overhang the edges. You can let a sticky focaccia dough rise directly on parchment paper, then set it right on the baking stone; wait about 10 minutes until the dough has set and pull out the parchment, leaving the dough to bake directly on the stone and develop a crispy crust. Be sure to trim the parchment paper so it doesn't overlap the sides of the stone; if it does, it will burn in the heat of the oven and you will find that your house smells of acrid smoke instead of the lovely aroma of freshly baked focaccia.

An *instant-read thermometer* will take the temperature of many things involved in home cooking and baking. It will record the internal temperature of the water for your yeast and tell you immediately if it is in the right range. Since yeast is activated at tempera-tures outside the strict parameters of 90° to 100°F for cake yeast and 105° to 115°F for active dry yeast, a certain amount of guesswork isn't fatal, but the thermometer can save you from disaster by alerting you when the liquid is so hot (over 140°F) that it will kill the yeast.

Tall straight-sided translucent *plastic refrigerator containers* or large *Pyrex glass measuring cups* are especially helpful for watching the dough rise. You can mark the exact level where the dough started and then easily tell when it has doubled.

A short-handled *baker's peel*, a thin, flat wooden paddle, is perfect for moving free-form focaccia and pizza in and out of the oven. Be sure to sprinkle it with cornmeal or flour before placing the dough on it so that it won't stick; once the dough has risen, a couple of good stiff shakes should free the focaccia to settle directly onto a cornmeal-sprinkled baking stone. Peels come in a variety of sizes; be sure that yours is at least 12 inches wide and fits easily inside the mouth of the oven. A rimless cookie sheet makes a good substitute.

A *pizza pan* with a perforated bottom helps dramat-ically in the shaping of very thin focaccia, since you can spread the dough directly in the pan instead of forming it freehand. It makes it easy to get a crispy crust, since heat from a baking stone makes direct contact with the exposed portions of the bottom sur-face of the dough. Brush the pan lightly with olive oil before placing the dough inside.

❧ I like to use a *wire whisk* for stirring the yeast into the water and for beating in the first cup of flour if I'm making focaccia by hand, so I don't get lumps in the dough.

❧ *Pastry brushes* spread olive oil evenly over the dough of a two-crusted focaccia and over the edges of regular *focacce*.

❧ A high-quality *serrated bread knife*, *sharp scissors*, or a *pizza cutter* makes slicing your focaccia a pleasure.

Temperature

The temperature of the dough and the room in which it rises governs the speed, quality, and timing of the fermentation. Bakers consider 75°F the ideal temperature of the room in which the dough rises and 75° to 78°F the ideal temperature of the dough at the end of the mixing and kneading. I've actually seen bakers whip out instant thermometers to take the temperature of the dough to be sure that it is in the correct range. If the dough rises too quickly, it will lose both flavor and structure.

❧ Have all your ingredients at room temperature. People who weigh the starter can use it at room temperature, but people who measure the starter with cup measures should scoop it from the refrigerator because the starter expands as it sits at room temperature. In the heat of summer you may want to refrigerate your flour and use cool water; in winter, you can warm the flour in a very low oven and and heat the water. If your dough is very warm—above 80°F—you may place it in a cool spot, such as a storeroom, basement, garage, or even in the refrigerator. If it is too cold, set the dough in a warm spot such as on a ledge 2 or 3 feet above a range top, on top of a turned-on clothes dryer, even under the blankets of a still warm bed.

How to make focaccia doughs

All the glorious rounds and rectangles of dough that become delicious *focacce* depend on that mysterious substance called yeast to rise and reach their full taste. I want to convince everyone—especially people with a fear of baking—that there's nothing to be afraid of in the harmless small granules that keep happily for months in their tiny sealed packets. All they need is a little moisture, some warmth, and food in the form of flour, and they return to life with dispatch.

❧ There are three ways to add yeast to doughs. The simplest and most direct is simply to place warm water in a small bowl, sprinkle the yeast over the top, and whisk it in until it dissolves. Active dry yeast comes vigorously back to life in water that is about 105° to 115°F, while cake yeast should be crumbled over slightly cooler—95° to 105°F—water. You can use an instant-read thermometer to allay your anxieties, but don't worry if your water isn't precisely that temperature. Do be careful that it is below 140°F, where yeast will die. Let the mixture stand until it is clearly creamy, about 5 to 10 minutes, then stir it to mix well.

Some recipes call for a sponge, which is simply a bit of the total dough made a short time before combining all the ingredients to give the final dough a preliminary boost. The yeast is dissolved in warm water, then a bit of flour is beaten in to make a smooth batter. In some cases sugar, milk, even eggs may be added. The bowl is covered with plastic wrap and the dough is allowed to stand until it becomes frothy and full of bubbles, anywhere from 20 minutes to 1 hour. The sponge is merely the first stage in making the true dough, which usually consists of a new infusion of yeast as well as water, flour, and other ingredients. Because the sponge ferments for such a short time, it does not produce the complex flavor or irregular texture developed by the prolonged fermentation of a starter.

A starter, called a *biga* in Italian, is essentially a mixture of water and flour combined with a tiny bit of yeast to make a very wet dough that is allowed to ferment for 6 to 24 hours before the baking begins. The starter allows a slow fermentation, which adds an additional rich taste and wheaty fragrance to the focaccia by accentuating the nutty taste of the grain. Italians use a starter in part because their flours are weak and need all the strength and help they can get. Our flours are wonderful, but any dough gains in moisture, full-bodied flavor, and complex porous structure from the secondary fermentation produced by the long slow rise of a starter. Italian bakers don't need to make a new starter every time they bake because they have fermented dough left from the previous day, but since home bakers can't count on such a resource, we need to make a starter and let it rise until it triples in volume and then falls back on itself. A starter can be kept for 1 day at room temperature and for 3 to 4 days in the refrigerator, or it can be frozen and then brought back to life at room temperature in a mere 3 hours. Make the starter at least 6 to 10 hours before you plan to start the final dough. Please weigh it if you plan to use it at room temperature because it expands as it warms. If you measure it directly from the refrigerator, it may slow your rising time slightly. The recipe makes more than you will need for almost any single focaccia recipe.

MIXING AND KNEADING DOUGH BY HAND: Most of the doughs in this book can be mixed and kneaded by hand. To make them, place the warm water in a small bowl and sprinkle the yeast over the top, whisking in the granules to be sure they dissolve. Stir the mixture well, transfer to a large mixing bowl, and blend in the rest of the wet ingredients. If there is a starter involved, chop it into small pieces or squeeze it through your fingers into the bowl. I use a whisk to mix the first cup of flour and the salt into the liquid mixture; thereafter, I use a wooden spoon to stir in the remaining flour to make the dough. All these recipes call for a specific amount of flour. Depending on how your flour absorbs moisture, you may not need all of the flour specified; as a precaution you may reserve the last 1/2 cup of flour until the end of the mixing.

Turn the mixture onto a lightly floured work surface and pat it into a flat disc. If the dough is moist and sticky, keep a pile of flour nearby to sprinkle sparingly over the top. Knead by lifting the far edge of the dough and folding it toward you. Use the heel of your hand to push the dough gently away from you by pressing it out, not down. Turn the dough 90 degrees and repeat the motion. If the dough is very sticky at first, use the dough scraper to lift the dough and fold it over. Be careful not to let the dough stick to the work surface, but if some does, use your dough scraper to scrape away the sticky portion; sprinkle the work surface with a little flour before you start kneading again. As you continue to knead you will feel the gluten developing as the dough becomes smoother and more resilient. You can pick up the ball of any firm focaccia dough after about 5 minutes and toss it down hard against the work surface several times to activate the gluten, but do not attempt the same technique with soft or sticky doughs. Please read the description of the texture of the final dough in each recipe. In all cases, I urge you to resist adding extra flour unless the dough seems excessively wet. Do not be afraid of ending up with a slightly sticky or moist dough. You can tell if you have kneaded the dough enough if it springs back when you press your finger into it.

MIXING AND KNEADING DOUGH WITH A MIXER: Please be sure to use a heavy-duty standing electric mixer such as a KitchenAid or Kenwood with two attachments: a paddle for mixing and a dough hook for kneading. Smaller machines are not up to the job and may burn out their motors. Knead at low (speed 2 on the KitchenAid) and medium (speed 4 on the KitchenAid) speed only; higher speeds are definitely not kind to doughs.

Pour the warm water right into the mixer bowl, sprinkle the yeast over the top, whisk it in, and let stand until creamy, about 5 to 10 minutes. Using the paddle attachment, stir in the rest of the liquids. If there is a starter, chop it up and add it to the bowl or squeeze it through your fingers directly into the bowl. Stir in the starter briefly until the mixture is chalky white. Add the flour and the salt and mix on low speed until a dough forms, about 1 to 3 minutes. Since flour amounts can vary according to how flour absorbs moisture, you may hold back $1/2$ cup of the flour until the end of the mixing. If the mixture is still wet and shaggy, gradually add whatever is needed of the remaining flour until a dough forms. Change to the dough hook and knead until the dough matches the description given in the recipe. If it seems too soft or wet, you may add a little extra flour, no more than 1 tablespoonful at a time, but since the dough does not always clear the side of the bowl in these recipes, you must be careful not to add too much. The dough is ready when it is resilient, responsive, and elastic. It should match the description of texture in each recipe. I always like to finish by kneading the dough briefly on a lightly floured work surface, then shaping the dough loosely into a ball.

MIXING AND KNEADING DOUGH WITH A FOOD PROCESSOR: Almost all of the focaccia doughs in this book may be made in a food processor. Instead of writing instructions in each recipe, I urge you to read this description and follow it each time. All doughs with a flour measurement of 3 3/4 cups (500 grams) may be made in a regular processor with a 6 1/2-inch-diameter bowl. Those with larger measurements or with a substantial amount of starter should be made in two batches and then combined in a single container for the rising.

❧ Because the heat of the motor and the speed of the processor can overheat a dough in no time, all the water, except the small amount used to dissolve the yeast, must be very cold, and the starter, if there is one, should be refrigerated until you are ready to use it. It is very easy to overknead a dough in a such a powerful machine, so set a timer and knead the dough for no longer than 25 to 40 seconds. It is much better to finish kneading on a lightly floured work surface than to overwork the dough.

❧ Place the dough blade or the steel blade in the processor bowl, add the flour and the salt, and pulse several times to mix them. Pour the warm water into a large measuring cup or pitcher with a spout, sprinkle the yeast over the surface, whisk it in to dissolve the granules, and let stand until creamy, about 5 to 10 minutes. Add the rest of the liquids, including a starter, if there is one, and, with the motor running, pour the wet ingredients down the feed tube and process just until they come together in a rough mass. To knead, process no longer than 25 to 40 seconds or, preferably, finish kneading by hand on a lightly floured work surface.

FIRST RISING: Choose a container large enough to permit the dough to double in volume. Although you may use ceramic, earthenware, or glass bowls, I recommend using a straight-sided translucent plastic container or a large glass beaker, such as a 2-quart Pyrex measuring cup, which allows you to mark the side where the dough starts its rise. It is then easy to monitor the process and know exactly when the dough has doubled. You can find large plastic containers at kitchenware or hardware stores. Lightly oil the inside of whichever container you are using, set the dough inside, cover tightly with plastic wrap, leave in a warm, draft-free spot, and let rise until doubled or as the recipe instructs.

SHAPING: Most focaccia doughs double in 1 to 2 hours. Regular unfilled focaccia doughs then are spread directly onto oiled baking sheets or pans. If the recipe calls for two or more *focacce,* divide the dough into equal pieces. To make a single focaccia, place the dough in an oiled baking pan and press it over the bottom as far as you can toward the edges. It is likely to resist after a bit, so cover it with a towel and let it rest for 10 minutes, then press it out farther until the dough reaches the edges.

To shape dough for filled focaccia, divide the dough in half, flatten each piece into a 1-inch-thick disc, and cover the piece of dough you are not using. Lightly flour the work surface and, with a lightly floured rolling pin, roll the dough until it is about $\frac{1}{8}$ to $\frac{1}{4}$ inch thick. Lay the dough in an oiled baking pan, making sure that some dough drapes over the edges. Lightly brush the dough with oil and spread the filling over the dough. Roll out the remaining piece of dough to form a circle with a diameter slightly larger than the pan and lay it over the filling. Trim the edges of any excess dough and, with your fingers, carefully pinch the edges of the two layers together tightly to seal them. Brush the top crust with oil and prick the surface with a fork.

To shape super-thin crusts for a flat focaccia using a rolling pin, place the dough on a lightly floured surface and sprinkle a very small amount of flour over the top. Using the heels of your hands, press the dough into a circle, then roll it out with a lightly floured rolling pin until it is about $\frac{1}{8}$ inch thick. Set the dough on a parchment paper–lined or cornmeal-dusted baker's peel or on an oiled perforated pizza pan, where you can press it out even thinner if you wish. Leave the rim a bit thicker than the interior.

To shape super-thin crusts for a flat focaccia by hand, divide the dough into the correct number of pieces and lightly flour your work surface. Flatten each piece into a disc and very lightly flour each side. It is especially easy if you set the dough on an oiled perforated pizza pan. Using the heels of your hands and starting from the center of the dough, stretch and press toward the edges, turning the dough constantly, all the while keeping it in the shape of a circle. Leave the rim a bit thicker than the interior of the dough.

SECOND RISING: Second rises are generally shorter than first rises. If the dough is to rise in a baking pan, be sure you have oiled it first; if it is to rise on a baker's peel, be sure you have sprinkled the surface with flour, cornmeal, or semolina. Parchment paper is wonderfully useful. You may shape a delicate focaccia dough and place it in an oiled baking pan lined with parchment paper. When the time comes for baking, the focaccia will bake directly on the parchment paper and then be easy to remove from the pan. Cover the dough with a kitchen towel and leave to rise again. A few *focacce* have 3 rises; most are made using a second rise in which the dough rests for 30 to 45 minutes before or just after being shaped.

BAKING: At least 30 minutes before you plan to bake, preheat the oven to 425°F with the optional baking stone, quarry tiles, or bricks on the lower or middle rack. Almost all *focacce* should be baked with moisture in the oven. Bakers in professional bakeries have ovens with steam injection, but home bakers must use a little ingenuity. To add moisture to the oven, spray cold water from a spritzer bottle onto the walls and floor of the oven 3 times during the first 10 minutes of baking. Spray quickly, close the door immediately to keep the steam in, and bake for 3 minutes. Repeat twice. Be careful to aim away from the electric light bulb, if there is one, because it might explode. Bake the focaccia until the dough is golden on top; use a spatula to pry up one edge to check that it is also golden underneath. If a recipe calls for more *focacce* than will fit comfortably in your oven at one time, work with one dough at a time and cover the other or others. Bake as directed and repeat the process with the remaining focaccia dough. Unless a recipe specifically recommends against it, immediately remove the focaccia from the pan and place on a rack to keep the bottom from getting soggy. Cool briefly. Eat focaccia warm or at room temperature; never refrigerate it.

SERVING AND STORING: Focaccia should be eaten the day it is made. However, I have discovered that a focaccia made with vegetables that have been sautéed in oil and laid in a thick layer across the top seems to keep well for a second day. The *focacce* from Puglia made with boiled potatoes in the dough keep better than those made without them. *Focacce* made only with flour, water, yeast, salt, and olive oil and perhaps some starter have the chewiness and texture of bread but also have the least keeping power. If you do decide to keep a focaccia overnight, place it in a plastic bag, close it tightly, and hope for the best.

FREEZING: To freeze focaccia dough, flatten the pieces into discs, wrap them tightly in plastic wrap, place in self-sealing plastic bags, and freeze for 3 to 4 months. You may thaw the dough in the refrigerator for 1 day, then bring it to room temperature or defrost it at a warm room temperature (75° to 80°F) in about 2 hours.

I have had limited success freezing baked focaccia, although I have had greater luck with filled *focacce* and with *focacce* paved with thick vegetable toppings. To freeze, wrap the focaccia tightly in aluminum foil, close tightly in a self-sealing bag, and freeze. Do not thaw. Remove from the plastic bag and set the foil-wrapped packet in a preheated 350°F oven for 20 to 25 minutes.

Four Basic Focaccia Doughs and One Starter

HOUGH THIS BOOK IS FULL OF INDIVIDUAL
focaccia recipes, each with its special flavor and taste, there are several doughs that can easily be used for a wide spectrum of toppings.

THE FIRST BASIC DOUGH IS MADE WITH A SPONGE, WHICH IS MERELY A LITTLE INFUSION OF yeast, water, and flour that gives the dough a head start and can also give you, the baker, some flexibility in your schedule. Having made this dough with and without the use of a sponge, I can assure you that a sponge adds a richness and depth of flavor. Please notice that you can make a sponge with a little bit of whole-wheat as well as with all unbleached white flour.

THE OIL- AND WINE-INFUSED DOUGH FROM GENOA PRODUCES AN AMAZINGLY FLAVORFUL focaccia. One local expert, who readily acknowledged the Genoans' reputation for extreme thriftiness, explained that wine, being plentiful, was added as a way of getting flavor without spending extra money. Even if it is apocryphal, this makes a good story, and the wine certainly does produce a remarkably delicious focaccia.

PEOPLE FAMILIAR WITH ITALIAN BAKING WILL RECOGNIZE THAT A STARTER, OR BIGA, IS simply a very bubbly wet mixture of flour, water, and a tiny bit of yeast left to rise until it triples and falls back on itself. Let it stand anywhere from 6 to 24 hours and use it immediately or refrigerate it for 3 or 4 days. Discard it after 5 days, or when it begins to go flat and ooze moisture. The basic starter on page 36 may be used in any recipe calling for a starter; it can be made ahead and refrigerated; and it may even be frozen and returned to life within 3 hours. A starter gives a lovely aroma and fragrance to focaccia doughs and is responsible as well for a slightly chewy texture. Please try baking focaccia dough with a starter to see what a remarkable difference in flavor, taste, and texture it can make.

Basic Focaccia
FOCACCIA

🍀

This basic focaccia dough and the Genoese dough that follows both have an extremely nice flavor and a slightly porous texture. They are easy to make and work well as basic doughs for many of the focacce in this book. If you would like this dough to rise more slowly, cut the yeast by half or even three quarters. You can make the dough, cover it well with plastic wrap, and place in the refrigerator for use later in the day. You can also make the dough one day and use it the next.

SPONGE

1 teaspoon active dry yeast

½ cup warm water, 105° to 115°F

¾ cup (100 grams) unbleached all-purpose flour

DOUGH

1 teaspoon active dry yeast

1 cup warm water, 105° to 115°F

3 tablespoons extra-virgin olive oil

Sponge, above

3¼ cups (450 grams) unbleached all-purpose flour

2 teaspoons sea salt

TOPPING

2 tablespoons extra-virgin olive oil

1 to 1¼ teaspoons coarse sea salt

🍃 To make the sponge: Sprinkle the yeast over the warm water in a large mixing or mixer bowl, whisk it in, and let stand until creamy, about 10 minutes. Stir in the flour. Cover tightly with plastic wrap and let rise until very bubbly and doubled, about 45 minutes.

🍃 To make the dough: Sprinkle the yeast over the warm water in a small bowl, whisk it in, and let stand until creamy, about 5 to 10 minutes. With a wooden spoon, stir the yeast mixture and olive oil into the sponge and mix well. If you are making the dough by hand, whisk in 1 cup of the flour; stir in the salt and remaining flour, 2 cups at a time, and mix until the dough is well blended. Knead on a lightly floured surface until soft and velvety, about 8 to 10 minutes.

🍃 If you are using a heavy-duty mixer, add the dissolved yeast and the olive oil to the sponge in the mixer bowl; mix in with the paddle attachment until well blended. Add the flour and salt and stir until thoroughly mixed, 1 to 2 minutes. Change to the dough hook and knead at medium speed until the dough is soft, velvety, and slightly sticky, 3 to 4 minutes. At this point you will be able to pull the dough up into peaks with your fingers. Finish by sprinkling 1 tablespoon of flour on your work surface and kneading the dough briefly until it comes together nicely.

🍃 First rise. Place the dough in a lightly oiled container, cover it tightly with plastic wrap, and let rise until doubled, 1¼ hours.

🍃 Shaping and second rise. The dough will be soft, delicate, and full of air bubbles. Flatten it on an oiled 11 x 17-inch baking pan and press it out with oiled or wet hands. Because the dough will be sticky and may not cover the bottom of the pan, cover it with a towel and let it relax for 10 minutes, then stretch it again until it reaches the edges. Cover with a towel and let rise for 45 minutes to 1 hour, or until the dough is full of air bubbles. Just before baking, dimple the dough vigorously with your knuckles or fingertips, leaving visible indentations. Drizzle olive oil over the dough, being sure some of the oil pools in the little holes you have made. Sprinkle with coarse sea salt.

❧ Baking. At least 30 minutes before you plan to bake, preheat the oven to 425°F with a baking stone inside if you have one. Place the focaccia pan directly on the stone and spray the oven walls and floor with cold water from a spritzer bottle 3 times during the first 10 minutes of baking. Bake until the crust is crisp and the top is golden, about 20 to 25 minutes. You may remove the focaccia from the pan and bake it directly on the baking stone for the last 10 minutes. Remove from the pan immediately and place on a rack. Serve warm or at room temperature.

❧ *Makes one 11 x 17-inch focaccia; serves 10 to 12*

Whole-Wheat Focaccia
FOCACCIA INTEGRALE

❦

Substituting ¾ cup of whole wheat-flour for an equivalent amount of unbleached flour in the dough produces a chewy rustic focaccia. Use it instead of the more citified basic dough for an earthier variation.

SPONGE
1 teaspoon active dry yeast
½ cup warm water, 105° to 115°F
¾ cup (100 grams) unbleached all-purpose flour

DOUGH
1 teaspoon active dry yeast
1 cup warm water, 105° to 115°F
3 tablespoons extra-virgin olive oil
Sponge, above
2½ cups (350 grams) unbleached all-purpose flour
¾ cup (100 grams) whole-wheat flour
2 teaspoons sea salt

TOPPING
2 tablespoons extra-virgin olive oil
1 to 1¼ teaspoons coarse sea salt

❧ To make the sponge: Sprinkle the yeast over the warm water in a large mixing or mixer bowl, whisk it in, and let stand until creamy, about 10 minutes. Stir in the flour. Cover tightly with plastic wrap and let rise until very bubbly and doubled, about 45 minutes.

❧ To make the dough: Sprinkle the yeast over the warm water in a small bowl, whisk it in, and let stand until creamy, about 5 to 10 minutes. With a wooden spoon, stir the yeast mixture and olive oil into the sponge and mix well. If you are making the dough by hand, whisk in 1 cup of the unbleached flour; stir in the salt and remaining flours, 1 cup at a time, and mix until the dough is well blended. Knead on a lightly floured surface until soft and velvety, about 8 to 10 minutes.

❧ If you are using a heavy-duty mixer, add the dissolved yeast and the olive oil to the sponge in the mixer bowl; mix in with the paddle attachment until well blended. Add the flours and salt and stir until thoroughly mixed, 1 to 2 minutes. Change to the dough hook and knead at medium speed until the dough is soft, velvety, and slightly sticky, 3 to 4 minutes. At this point you will be able to pull the dough up into peaks with your fingers. Finish by sprinkling 1 tablespoon of flour on your work surface and kneading the dough briefly until it comes together nicely.

❧ First rise. Place the dough in a lightly oiled container, cover it tightly with plastic wrap, and let rise until doubled, 1¼ hours.

❧ Shaping and second rise. The dough will be soft, delicate, and full of air bubbles. Flatten it on an oiled 11 x 17-inch baking pan and press it out with oiled or wet hands. Because the dough will be sticky and may not cover the bottom of the pan, cover it with a towel and let it relax for 10 minutes, then stretch it again until it reaches the edges. Cover with a towel and let rise for 45 minutes to 1 hour, or until the dough is full of air bubbles. Just before baking, dimple the dough vigorously with your knuckles or fingertips, leaving visible indentations. Drizzle olive oil over the dough, being sure some of the oil pools in the little holes you have made. Sprinkle with coarse sea salt.

❧ Baking. At least 30 minutes before you plan to bake, preheat the oven to 425°F with a baking stone inside if you have one. Place the focaccia pan directly on the stone and spray the oven walls and floor with cold water from a spritzer bottle 3 times during the first 10 minutes of baking. Bake until the crust is crisp and the top is golden, about 20 to 25 minutes. You may remove the focaccia from the pan and bake it directly on the baking stone for the last 10 minutes. Remove from the pan immediately and place on a rack. Serve warm or at room temperature.

❧ *Makes one 11 x 17-inch focaccia; serves 10 to 12*

Focaccia from Genoa
FOCACCIA AL'OLIO

❦

The focacce of Genoa are as various as the bakers who make them, but the haunting flavor of this particular dough makes it eminently clear why the city is so famous for its flat bread. It's hard to get enough of this focaccia al'olio, which combines water, wine, and olive oil and has a delicate taste and a light porous texture. Anything else? There's something unforgettable about the crunch of the crust.

SPONGE
2½ teaspoons (1 package) active dry yeast
⅔ cup warm water, 105° to 115°F
1 cup (140 grams) unbleached all-purpose flour

DOUGH

½ cup water, room temperature

⅓ cup dry white wine

⅓ cup light extra-virgin olive oil, preferably Ligurian

Sponge, above

2½ cups plus 2 teaspoons (360 grams) unbleached all-
    purpose flour, plus 1 to 2 tablespoons as needed

2 teaspoons sea salt

TOPPING

About 2 tablespoons extra-virgin olive oil, preferably
    Ligurian

¾ to 1 teaspoon sea salt

❧ To make the sponge: Sprinkle the yeast over the warm water in a large mixing bowl, whisk it in, and let stand until creamy, about 10 minutes. Stir in the flour and beat until smooth. Cover tightly with plastic wrap and let rise until puffy and bubbling, about 30 minutes.

❧ To make the dough: Add the water, wine, and olive oil to the sponge. If you are making the dough by hand, whisk in 1 cup of flour and the salt, then beat in the rest of the flour until you have a dough that is very soft and very sticky. Knead on a lightly floured board with the help of a dough scraper and 1 to 2 additional table-spoons of flour for 6 to 8 minutes, or until the dough comes together nicely and is silky and shiny; it should remain soft but not wet.

❧ If you are using a heavy-duty mixer, set the paddle attachment in place and add the water, wine, and olive oil to the sponge. Add the flour and salt and mix until the dough comes together while remaining very soft. Change to the dough hook and knead for 3 minutes at medium speed, stopping once or twice to press the

dough into a ball to aid in the kneading. Use the 1 to 2 tablespoons additional flour if you finish by kneading the dough briefly on a lightly floured work surface.

❧ First rise. Place the dough in a lightly oiled container, cover it tightly with plastic wrap, and let rise until doubled, about 1 hour.

❧ Shaping and second rise. The dough should be soft, full of air bubbles, and stretch easily. Press it into a lightly oiled 10½ x 15½-inch pan, dimple it well with your fingertips or knuckles, cover with a towel, and let rise until puffy and doubled, about 45 minutes.

❧ Baking. At least 30 minutes before you plan to bake, preheat the oven to 425°F with a baking stone inside, if you have one. Once again dimple the top of the dough with your fingertips or knuckles, drizzle olive oil so it pools in the little indentations, and sprinkle with the sea salt. Place the focaccia pan directly on the stone and immediately reduce the temperature it to 400°F, spraying the oven walls and floor with cold water from a spritzer bottle 3 times in the first 10 minutes. Bake the focaccia for 25 to 30 minutes, until golden. Immediately remove from the pan and let cool on a rack. Serve warm or at room temperature.

❧ *Makes one 10½ x 15½-inch focaccia; serves 10 or 12*

Starter for Focaccia
BIGA
❀

There's nothing complicated about making a starter, or biga, which is merely a tiny amount of yeast mixed with water and flour and left to rise and mellow at a cool room temperature while a long, slow fermentation takes place. Scoop up some starter, stir it into a focaccia dough, and you'll find you've enhanced the flavor with an added fragrance, complexity, and depth of taste. The starter will keep for 3 to 4 days in the refrigerator, becoming sourer and tangier as time passes. You may freeze it for later use, or discard it after 5 days.

> ½ teaspoon active dry yeast
> ¼ cup warm water, 105° to 115°F
> 1¼ cups plus 2 tablespoons water, room temperature
> 3¾ cups (500 grams) unbleached all-purpose flour

❧ Sprinkle the yeast over the warm water in a large mixing or mixer bowl, whisk it in, and let stand until creamy, about 10 minutes. Stir in the remaining water and then the flour, mixing with a wooden spoon for about 100 strokes or with the paddle attachment of a heavy-duty mixer for 1 to 2 minutes until a sticky dough is formed.

❧ Rising. You may leave the dough in the mixing bowl or transfer it to a lightly oiled bowl. Cover it tightly with plastic wrap and let rise at cool room temperature for 6 to 24 hours. The starter will triple in volume and then collapse upon itself. It will still be bubbly, wet, and sticky when ready to use. Cover and refrigerate after 24 hours. When needed, scoop out the desired amount. This recipe can easily be doubled.

❧ Makes 3½ cups

Schiacciata with Starter
SCHIACCIATA CON BIGA
❀

Here's proof of the power of a starter: The incredible flavor of the grain, the porous texture of the dough, and the fragrance in this schiacciata all come from a biga. I would recommend making it with the best stone-ground organically grown flour you can find. Don't forget to measure your starter by weight if at all possible. If you want this dough to fit into your schedule, you can let it rise in the refrigerator overnight; just cut the amount of yeast to ½ teaspoon and measure the starter cold, and you'll find that a long, slow rise will bring out even more flavor.

> DOUGH
> ¾ teaspoon active dry yeast
> 1½ cups warm water, 105° to 115°F
> 7 tablespoons (100 grams) Starter for Focaccia
>   no more than 2 days old
> 2½ tablespoons extra-virgin olive oil
> 3¾ cups (500 grams) unbleached all-purpose flour,
>   preferably organically grown and stone-ground
> 1½ teaspoons sea salt

TOPPING
2 tablespoons extra-virgin olive oil
¾ to 1 teaspoon coarse sea salt
Freshly ground black pepper, optional

❧ Whisk the yeast into the warm water in a large mixing or mixer bowl and let stand until creamy, about 10 minutes. Chop up or squeeze the starter through your fingers into the bowl and stir in the olive oil. If you are making the dough by hand, combine the flour and the salt and stir them into the yeast mixture in 2 additions. Knead on a lightly floured surface for 8 to 10 minutes, or until velvety, moist, and slightly sticky.

❧ If you are using a heavy-duty electric mixer, stir in the flour and salt with the paddle attachment and mix for 2 minutes. Change to the dough hook and knead for 5 minutes on low speed, or until the dough is velvety and moist but not sticky.

❧ First rise. Place the dough in a lightly oiled container, cover tightly with plastic wrap, and let rise until doubled, about 1½ hours.

❧ Shaping and second rise. You may divide the dough into 3 equal pieces and spread each in an oiled 9-inch pie pan, or you may moisten your hands and spread all the dough on an oiled 11 x 17-inch baking pan. Cover with towels and let rise until doubled, about 2 hours.

❧ Third rise: At least 30 minutes before you plan to bake, preheat the oven to 425°F with a baking stone inside, if you have one. Dimple the dough with vigor—it is very responsive—drizzle it with 1½ tablespoons olive oil, and sprinkle with coarse salt and the optional freshly ground black pepper; leave for 30 minutes.

❧ Baking. Just before baking, sprinkle the remaining oil over the top of the *schiacciata*—don't be hesitant or sparing. Place the focaccia pan directly on the baking stone. Bake for 5 minutes, then reduce the temperature to 400°F, spraying the oven walls and floor with cold water from a spritzer bottle 3 times in the first 10 minutes. Continue baking until the *schiacciata* is golden brown on top and underneath (check by lifting one corner with a spatula), about 20 to 25 minutes. Immediately remove from the pan and place on a rack. Serve warm or at room temperature.

❧ *Makes one 11 x 17-inch schiacciata or three 9-inch round schiacciate; serves 10 to 12*

SAVORY FOCACCIA

FOCACCIA WITH ROSEMARY, FOCACCIA WITH sage, focaccia with a mosaic of olives, a sprinkling of herbs, a carpet of caramelized onions: All of the most fragrant ingredients from the countryside find their way into focaccia, either scattered in its interior or sprinkled over the top of glorious doughs. Traditional *focacce* appear on the Italian table as part of the ceremony of everyday life, for this is the food that has fed and comforted the people of Italy for centuries. Many of them depend on the produce of the fields—succulent sweet peppers, fragrant basil and oregano, tiny meaty tomatoes called *pomodorini*—some rely on olives that have been cured in oil, preserved in brine, or turned into olive paste, others use walnuts plucked from trees, or anchovies and sardines fished out of the sea. All these are part of a great panoply of ingredients that dapple the top of delicious doughs and become a variant of people's daily bread.

SOME OF THE FOLLOWING FOCACCE COME FROM OTHER MEDITERRANEAN COUNTRIES: One is from Provence, which was once part of Italy when Nice was known as Nizza, and another from Majorca, a Spanish outpost with Roman historical roots. Some are made with common white flour, others with the earthy flavor of whole wheat or the crunch of cornmeal, and still others depend on ancient grains like spelt, or *farro,* and durum that grow on the fertile Tavoliere plain of Puglia and have now found their way to America.

A FEW OF THESE FOCACCE ARE PRODUCTS OF MY FANTASIA, A LEAP OF IMAGINATION that blends an ancient idea with new pairings of ingredients. I've never actually come across a sun-dried tomato focaccia in the canon, and I admit to dreaming up the focaccia dappled with Gorgonzola, red onions, and walnuts by combining three Italian ingredients that are both common and sublime. I couldn't resist taking very old grains like spelt, which is newly available, and brand-new flours, like white wheat from red grain, and making *focacce* that are variants of ancient recipes. All of them are food for the senses: for the eyes, the tastebuds, the tongue, and the fingers. Eat them informally with friends and family, spread them across a table with antipasti and salads, make a meal of them with a frittata or an omelet. Set them forth with a glass of wine and sing the praises of focaccia.

Basil-topped Focaccia
FOCACCIA AL BASILICO
❦

What could be simpler or more charming than this traditional focaccia made in the hills of Liguria and the unspoiled green countryside of the Garfagnana in western Tuscany? In the time when country women still baked once a week, they used to tuck a single basil leaf into each dimple and declivity on the surface of their focaccia. Such simple alchemy creates an engaging pattern to delight the eye, while the aroma of basil dances on the air and tickles the senses.

DOUGH
Basic Focaccia (page 32) or Focaccia from Genoa dough (page 34), made through the second rise
TOPPING
1¼ to 1½ tablespoons olive oil
¾ to 1 teaspoon coarse sea salt
35 to 50 fresh basil leaves

❧ Prepare the focaccia dough through the second rise. Preheat the oven as directed to 425°F with a baking stone inside, if you are using one. Just before baking, dimple the top with your knuckles and drizzle it with olive oil, being sure to make pronounced holes to trap a small pool of the oil in each one. Sprinkle with sea salt.

❧ Set the focaccia pan directly on the baking stone and spray the oven walls and floor with cold water from a spritzer bottle 3 times during the first 10 minutes of baking. Bake the focaccia until the top is pale golden, about 25 minutes. Remove the focaccia from the oven and press a single basil leaf into each indentation. Immediately remove from the pan and place on a rack. Serve warm or at room temperature.

❧ Makes one 11 x 17-inch or one 10½ x 15½-inch focaccia; serves 10 to 12

Focaccia with Rosemary, Oil, and Salt
FOCACCIA AL ROSMARINO
❦

As traditional a focaccia as exists in Italy, this crunchy rectangle of dough is made fragrant with fresh rosemary leaves that dapple both its interior and surface. Be certain to dimple the top well, to drizzle it with extra-virgin olive oil, and to sprinkle it liberally with crystals of coarse sea salt.

DOUGH
Basic Focaccia dough (page 32)
3 tablespoons finely chopped fresh rosemary leaves
TOPPING
About 1¼ to 1½ tablespoons extra-virgin olive oil
¾ to 1 teaspoon coarse sea salt
Sprigs of fresh rosemary

❧ Prepare the basic focaccia dough, adding the chopped rosemary during the initial mixing. Proceed with the recipe, preheating the oven as directed to 425°F with a baking stone inside, if you have one. Just before baking, dimple the top of the dough with your knuckles and drizzle it with olive oil, being sure some of the oil is trapped in the little declivities you have made. Sprinkle with sea salt and press the rosemary sprigs into the dough.

❧ Set the focaccia pan directly on the baking stone and spray the oven walls and floor 3 times with cold water from a spritzer bottle during the first 10 minutes of baking, being careful not to hit the electric bulb if there is one. Bake until the crust is crisp and the top golden, about 20 to 25 minutes. Remove from the pan immediately and place on a rack. Serve warm or at room temperature.

❧ *Makes one 11 x 17-inch focaccia; serves 10 to 12*

Focaccia with Olive Paste

FOCACCIA AL PURÈ DI OLIVE NERE

✿

Black olives grow in such profusion in Liguria that many are crushed into a paste known as "poor man's caviar." You can buy olive paste at specialty gourmet shops, but if you decide to puree your own, you can make it fine or coarse depending on your taste, and you may spice it up with anchovies, capers, or herbs, if you like. Whichever way you choose, plunge the paste right into the dough to make a focaccia marbled with the dark rich flavor of olives.

DOUGH

Focaccia from Genoa dough (page 34), made through the first rise

¼ cup black olive paste

TOPPING

Extra-virgin olive oil

Pinch of sea salt

¼ cup finely chopped fresh flat-leaf parsley (optional)

❧ At the end of the first rise, turn the soft, stretchy dough onto a very lightly floured work surface, flatten it, and spread the black olive paste over the center. Knead the paste delicately into the dough. Spread the dough as directed into the lightly oiled 10½ x 15½-inch baking pan, dimple it with your fingertips, cover it with a towel, and let it rise as directed.

❧ Preheat the oven as directed to 400°F with a baking stone inside, if you have one. Dimple the dough firmly and drizzle oil over the top of the little indentations. Sprinkle with a very little bit of salt since the olive paste is salty itself. Bake the focaccia as directed, remove it immediately from the pan, and place on a rack. Decorate with the optional finely chopped parsley. Serve warm or at room temperature.

❧ *Makes one 10½ x 15½-inch focaccia; serves 10 to 12*

Provençale Focaccia
PISSALADIÈRE
❧

Here's a Provençale focaccia that migrated over the Italian border and now calls the nearby province of Imperia home.

DOUGH
Focaccia from Genoa dough (page 34), set out for the
   first rise
TOPPING
3 white onions, quartered
Extra-virgin olive oil
Sea salt

❧ While the dough is rising, make the onion topping. Place the white onions in abundant boiling water and boil for 2 to 3 minutes. Drain thoroughly, pat dry, and cool.

❧ Press the dough as directed into a lightly oiled 10½ x 15½-inch baking pan, dimple it well with your fingertips or knuckles, sprinkle it with abundant olive oil, and distribute the onions over the top. Cover with a towel and let rise until puffy, about 45 minutes.

❧ Baking. At least 30 minutes before you plan to bake, preheat the oven to 425°F with a baking stone inside, if you have one. Drizzle a little more olive oil over any parts of the dough that look dry, sprinkle salt over the top, and set the focaccia pan directly on the stone. Immediately reduce the temperature to 400°F, spray the oven walls and floor with cold water from a spritzer bottle 3 times during the first 10 minutes, and bake for 25 to 30 minutes, or until golden. Immediately remove from the pan and place on a rack. Serve warm or at room temperature.

❧ Makes one 10½ x 15½-inch focaccia; serves 10 to 12

Focaccia Andrea Doria
FOCACCIA ANDREA DORIA
❧

If you wonder how this focaccia, which is also called pizza all'Andrea, got its name, the popular explanation is that it was named for the favorite food of Admiral Andrea Doria, the most famous citizen of the town of Imperia, where it is made. Some experts demur and insist that it comes from the French patois for pissaladière or pissala, a pungent paste made of anchovies and sardines, as the onions in the original focaccia were prepared by being wrapped in a cloth that was dipped into the fishy paste. It isn't hard to see how pissaladière could turn into pizza all'Andrea and then be mistakenly connected to the admiral. In either case, this delicious focaccia was perfected in the nineteenth century when the tomato came to Liguria. Don't use Kalamata or Gaeta olives because they are too strong for this Ligurian specialty.

DOUGH

Focaccia from Genoa dough (page 34), set out for the first rise

TOPPING

4 tablespoons olive oil

1 white onion, finely chopped

2 pounds ripe tomatoes, peeled, seeded, and roughly chopped

2 fresh basil leaves, torn

5 anchovies preserved in salt, cleaned, washed well, bone removed, and cut into tiny pieces

2 garlic cloves, finely sliced

Black olives in brine, niçoise or Taggia type, pitted

4 teaspoons dried oregano

2 tablespoons olive oil

Pinch of sea salt

❧ While the dough is rising, warm 2 tablespoons of the olive oil in a heavy skillet or sauté pan over medium heat and sauté the onion until golden, about 10 minutes. Add the tomatoes and cook over medium-high heat until the liquid has almost entirely evaporated. Stir in the torn basil leaves and set aside to cool.

❧ Shaping and second rise. Stretch the puffy dough to fit an oiled 11 x 17-inch baking pan. Dimple the dough with your fingertips and spread the tomato topping over it. Cover with a towel and let rise until puffy, about 45 minutes.

❧ Baking. Thirty minutes before you plan to bake, preheat the oven to 400°F with a baking stone inside, if you have one. Just before baking, sprinkle the anchovies, garlic, olives, and oregano over the top of the dough and press them in with the back of a spoon. Drizzle with the remaining 2 tablespoons of olive oil, sprinkle the salt over the top, and spray the oven walls

and floor with cold water from a spritzer bottle 3 times in the first 10 minutes. Bake until the crust is golden, about 25 minutes. Immediately remove from the pan and cool briefly on a rack. Serve warm or at room temperature.

❧ *Makes one 10½ x 15½-inch focaccia; serves 8 to 10*

ANCHOVY-FLAVORED FOCACCIA (*SARDENARIA*): Yet another variation on a Ligurian theme comes from San Remo. This focaccia was named for sailors who went to Sardinia. Use 1 to 2 teaspoons anchovy paste in the tomato and onion base instead of the anchovies preserved in salt.

Whole-Wheat Focaccia with Olive Paste

FOCACCIA INTEGRALE AL PURÈ DI OLIVE

❀

*W*hole wheat and black olive paste make a deep and earthy focaccia. If you have olive paste left over, spread it on crostini or toss it with strands of pasta. Be sparing with salt in this dough since olives are already quite salty.

DOUGH

1¼ teaspoons active dry yeast

1¼ cups warm water, 105° to 115°F

1 tablespoon olive oil

2 tablespoons black olive paste

2½ cups (350 grams) stone-ground whole-wheat flour, plus 2 tablespoons as needed

1 teaspoon sea salt

2 teaspoons black olive paste

3 tablespoons olive oil, plus more for drizzling

Sea salt

Olive oil

3 tablespoons finely chopped fresh flat-leaf parsley

❧ Sprinkle the yeast over the warm water in a large mixing or mixer bowl, whisk it in, and let stand until creamy, about 10 minutes. If you are making the dough by hand, stir in the olive oil and black olive paste, then the 2½ cups of flour and salt in 2 additions, and mix well until the dough comes together. You may need to add 2 tablespoons more whole-wheat flour to get a good texture. Knead on a lightly floured work surface for 8 to 10 minutes.

❧ If you are using a heavy-duty electric mixer, set the paddle attachment in place and stir the olive oil and black olive paste into the yeast mixture. Add the flour and salt and mix well until a dough has formed. Change to the dough hook and knead for 1 to 2 minutes on low speed, then 4 to 5 on medium speed, or until the dough is soft, pliable, and elastic.

❧ First rise. Place the dough in a lightly oiled bowl, cover tightly with plastic wrap, and let rise until doubled, 45 minutes to 1 hour. The dough should be slightly sticky, firm, and responsive.

❧ Shaping and second rise. Press the dough into a well-oiled 10-inch round pie pan and spread it to fit the bottom of the pan. Cover it with a moist towel and let rise until doubled, about 1 hour.

❧ Baking. At least 30 minutes before you plan to bake, preheat the oven to 400°F with a baking stone inside,

if you have one. Just before baking, dimple the top of the focaccia with your knuckles. Blend the olive paste and the 3 tablespoons of olive oil in a small bowl and paint the mixture over the dough, being sure to press it into the holes. Sprinkle a tiny bit of salt over the top of the focaccia and drizzle it with a ribbon of olive oil that covers the edges and exposed portions of the dough. Place the pan directly on the stone and bake the focaccia for 22 to 25 minutes, or until golden, spraying the oven walls and floor with cold water from a spritzer bottle 3 times in the first 10 minutes. A minute or two before you take the focaccia out of the oven, sprinkle the chopped parsley over the top. Remove the focaccia from the pan and place on a rack. Serve warm or at room temperature.

❧ *Makes one 10-inch round focaccia; serves about 6*

Focaccia with a Mosaic of Olives
FOCACCIA ALLE OLIVE

❦

Imagine splitting this olive-studded focaccia in half and making it into a sandwich filled with lamb, roasted chicken, or with a tangle of glossy sautéed sweet red peppers. Here's food for lunch (just toss a salad on the side) or for an extraordinary picnic. One word of caution: don't use Kalamata or Gaeta olives, because they are too salty.

DOUGH

Focaccia from Genoa (page 34) or Basic Focaccia dough (page 32), made through the second rise

48 small black olives in brine (13 ounces), such as Taggia
    or niçoise variety
1 tablespoon olive oil
Pinch of sea salt
¼ cup finely chopped fresh flat-leaf parsley

❧ While the dough is rising, pit the olives by whacking them with the flat side of a cleaver, then slipping the pits out of the soft flesh. Split the olives roughly in half. Preheat the oven to 400°F with a baking stone inside, if you have one.

❧ Just before baking, press the olives into the top of the dough so that they make a pattern that looks like an elegantly designed mosaic. Drizzle the dough with oil and sprinkle it with a pinch of salt. Place the pan directly on the stone and bake the focaccia as directed for 20 to 25 minutes, or until golden, spraying the oven walls and floor with cold water from a spritzer bottle 3 times in the first 10 minutes. When done, immediately remove the focaccia from the pan and set on a rack. Brush the edges of the focaccia with olive oil, sprinkle the chopped parsley over the top, and serve warm or at room temperature.

❧ Makes one 10½ x 15½ focaccia; serves 8 to 10

Focaccia with Fresh Sage
FOCACCIA ALLA SALVIA
❧

From Ventimiglia to Lerici in the boomerang-shaped region of Liguria, the dramatically terraced countryside is dotted with the silvery green of olive trees, the dusty green of sage leaves, the soft green of marjoram, and a brilliant blaze of basil, the traditional tastes and colors of the region. The pungent flavor of downy sage leaves infuses the focaccia, making itself at home and leaving a distinctive Ligurian signature.

DOUGH
Focaccia from Genoa dough (page 34)
20 to 24 fresh sage leaves, finely chopped
TOPPING
About 1½ tablespoons extra-virgin olive oil
¾ to 1 teaspoon coarse sea salt
8 to 10 whole fresh sage leaves for decoration

❧ Prepare the focaccia dough, stirring the chopped sage leaves into the dough in the initial mixing. Proceed with the recipe through the baking by preheating the oven to 400°F with a baking stone inside, if you have one. Immediately upon removing the focaccia from the oven, transfer it from the pan to a rack and decorate the top with the whole sage leaves. Serve warm or at room temperature.

❧ Makes one 10½ x 15½-inch focaccia; serves 8 to 10

Whole-Wheat Schiacciata
SCHIACCIATA INTEGRALE
❋

When I first tasted a slice of this thin, chewy schiacciata in Florence, I was struck by its remarkable crunchiness. Italians intentionally mill some of their whole-wheat flour with the bran still in it, and this recipe depends on finding such a coarsely ground organic flour. Here is one time when a scale is particularly useful: Measure the flour carefully by weight, if you can, to produce a dough that remains slightly soft so it can really absorb the imprint of your fingertips. Similarly, it is best to weigh the starter, but if you can't, be sure to measure it straight from the refrigerator.

DOUGH

1¼ teaspoons active dry yeast

¼ cup warm water, 105° to 115°F

1¼ cups plus 1 tablespoon water, room temperature

2 tablespoons olive oil

½ cup plus 1 tablespoon (125 grams) Starter for Focaccia (page 000)

3¾ cups (500 grams) coarsely ground whole-wheat flour

1½ teaspoons sea salt

¼ cup finely chopped fresh marjoram (optional)

TOPPING

3 tablespoons olive oil

Coarse sea salt

Freshly ground black pepper

❧ Sprinkle the yeast over the warm water in a large mixing bowl, whisk it in, and let stand until creamy, about 10 minutes. Stir in the room-temperature water and the olive oil. If you are making this by hand, chop up the starter or squeeze it through your fingers and add it to the mixture in the bowl. Use a wooden spoon to stir in the 3 cups of flour, 1 cup at a time; add the remaining flour, the salt, and the optional marjoram and mix until the dough comes together. Knead on a lightly floured surface, using as little extra whole-wheat flour as you can, for about 5 or 6 minutes.

❧ If you are using a heavy-duty electric mixer, you can add the starter directly to the yeast mixture and mix it with the paddle attachment. Add the flour, salt, and optional marjoram and mix for 3 minutes. Change to the dough hook and knead for 3 minutes at medium speed. The dough will be coarse, slightly sticky, and elastic; you will really be able to feel the grittiness of the bran in the flour.

❧ First rise. Place the dough in a lightly oiled container, cover it tightly with plastic wrap, and let rise until doubled, about 1½ to 1¾ hours.

❧ Shape and Second rise. Place the dough on a well oiled 11 x 17-inch baking pan and stretch the dough toward the edges. If it doesn't quite reach, cover it with a towel, leave for 10 minutes, and stretch it again. Press your index fingers firmly into the dough, leaving clear indentations, then cover it with a towel and let rise until puffy and doubled, about 1 hour. Before baking, press your fingers firmly into the indentations again to make sure that they are deep and clear, drizzle the oil over the top so that little pools of it dapple the surface, and sprinkle with a bit of fine sea salt and freshly ground pepper.

❧ Baking. At least 30 minutes before you plan to bake, preheat the oven to 425°F with a baking stone inside, if you have one. Set the focaccia pan directly on the stone and spray the oven walls and floor 3 times with cold water from a spritzer bottle in the first 10 minutes. Bake for 5 minutes and then reduce the temperature to 400°F. Bake until the focaccia is browned on top and golden on the bottom, about 18 to 20 minutes. Immediately remove the focaccia from the pan and blot on paper towels if the bottom seems oily. Place on a rack. Serve warm or at room temperature.

❦ *Makes one 11 x 17-inch focaccia; serves 10 to 12*

Focaccia with Garlic and Tomatoes
FOCACCIA AL'AGLIO E POMODORI

❀

If you asked most people to describe a focaccia, I imagine they might choose this one with its wash of garlic and ripe tomatoes painted across the dimpled surface of the dough. Versatile and satisfying by itself, it is also delicious sliced and filled with soft cheeses or a tangle of sautéed greens.

DOUGH
Basic Focaccia (page 32) or Focaccia from Genoa dough
(page 34), set out for the second rise

TOPPING
2 tablespoons extra-virgin olive oil
1 clove garlic, minced
1 pound juicy ripe tomatoes, peeled and chopped, or one
  14-ounce can plum tomatoes, drained and chopped
¾ to 1 teaspoon coarse sea salt

❦ While the focaccia is rising, warm the olive oil over low heat in a medium heavy skillet or sauté pan, add the garlic and, after a minute or two, the tomatoes. Simmer gently over medium heat for 5 or 6 minutes, or until the tomatoes have cooked down and concentrated a bit. Set aside to cool.

❦ Baking. Just before baking, dimple the focaccia firmly and paint the top of the dough with the tomato mixture. Sprinkle the sea salt over the surface. Place the focaccia pan directly on the stone and spray the oven walls and floor with cold water from a spritzer bottle 3 times in the first 10 minutes. Bake until the top of the focaccia is golden, about 20 to 25 minutes. Immediately slide the focaccia out of the pan and place on a rack. Serve warm or at room temperature.

❦ *Makes one 11 x 17-inch or 10½ x 15½-inch focaccia; serves 10 to 12*

Focaccia with Garlic and Herbs
FOCACCIA AL'AGLIO, ROSMARINO, E SALVIA

❀

A simple focaccia, flavored only with garlic and herbs, is as easy to make as it is satisfying to eat.

1 recipe Basic Focaccia dough (page 32), made through the
    first rise

TOPPING

3 tablespoons best-quality extra-virgin olive oil
3 garlic cloves, sliced extremely thin
1 tablespoon chopped fresh rosemary leaves
1 tablespoon chopped fresh sage leaves
1½ to 2 teaspoons coarse sea salt

❧ While the dough is rising, make the garlic and herb topping: Warm the olive oil over low heat in a small sauté pan or heavy skillet, add the garlic, and sauté for 2 to 3 minutes without allowing it to change color. Swirl in the herbs and steep for another minute or two. Set aside to cool.

❧ Shaping and second rise. Flatten the dough in an oiled 11 x 17-inch baking pan and stretch and press it out with your hands to cover as much of the bottom as possible. Because it is sticky and may not cover the bottom of the pan, cover the dough with a towel and let it relax for 10 minutes, then stretch it again until it reaches the edges. Cover and let rise for 45 minutes to 1 hour, or until it is full of bubbles.

❧ Baking. Preheat the oven to 400°F as directed with a baking stone inside, if you have one. Just before baking, dimple the focaccia firmly and brush or drizzle the topping over the dough, encouraging it to settle in the little holes left by your fingertips. Sprinkle the sea salt over the surface. Set the focaccia pan directly on the stone and spray the oven walls and floor with cold water from a spritzer bottle 3 times in the first 10 minutes. Bake as directed until the focaccia is golden, 20 to 25 minutes. Remove the focaccia from the pan and place on a rack. Serve warm or at room temperature.

❧ Makes one 11 x 17-inch focaccia; serves 10 to 12

Focaccia from Pistoia
COFACCIA

❀

Pistoia is the only place in Italy where focaccia is called by the charming name of cofaccia. It is a country person's term for a delicious firm and chewy focaccia with a somewhat open interior texture. Cofaccia is traditionally flavored with oil and salt, but you can add a handful of chopped sage leaves to the dough and decorate the top with a few whole ones.

DOUGH

1¼ teaspoons active dry yeast
½ cup plus 3 tablespoons warm milk, 105° to 115°F
½ cup plus 3 tablespoons water, room temperature
¼ cup extra-virgin olive oil
3 cups and 2 tablespoons (450 grams) unbleached
    all-purpose flour
1½ teaspoons sea salt
10 to 12 fresh sage leaves, finely chopped (optional)

1 ½ to 2 tablespoons extra-virgin olive oil

¾ to 1 teaspoon coarse sea salt

6 to 8 whole fresh sage leaves for decorating (optional)

❧ Sprinkle the yeast over the warm milk in a small bowl, whisk it in, and let stand until creamy, about 10 minutes. Transfer the mixture to a large mixing or mixer bowl. If you are making the dough by hand, stir in the water and 2 tablespoons of the olive oil with a wooden spoon. Whisk in 1 cup of the flour, the sea salt, and the optional chopped sage leaves; add the remaining flour in 2 additions and stir with a wooden spoon until the dough comes together, 1 to 2 minutes. Knead on a lightly floured work surface for 8 to 10 minutes, or until silky, tender, and elastic.

❧ If you are using a heavy-duty mixer, use the paddle attachment to mix the flour, salt, and optional chopped sage leaves into the yeast mixture for 1 to 2 minutes. Change to the dough hook and knead for 4 minutes on low speed. The dough should clear the sides of the bowl but never quite pull away from the bottom. It will be silky, tender, elastic, and slightly sticky; move it to a lightly floured work surface and knead it briefly to make it firm and easy to handle.

❧ First rise. Place the dough in a lightly oiled container, cover it tightly with plastic wrap, and let rise until doubled, about 1 hour and 15 to 30 minutes.

❧ Shaping. Flour the work surface very lightly. Divide the dough into 3 equal pieces, shape each into a ball, cover with a towel and let relax for 10 to 15 minutes. Place each ball in the bottom of an oiled 9-inch pie pan and spread with your fingertips to cover the bottom. You may also place the balls of dough on 2 large baker's peels or on 2 rimless baking sheets lined with parchment paper. Pummel the tops with your fingertips or knuckles and drizzle 2 tablespoons of olive oil over them.

❧ Second rise. Cover the dough with towels and let rise until puffy and half risen, about 30 minutes. Dimple the tops again to make sure that the oil remains in the holes; sprinkle with the coarse sea salt.

❧ Baking. At least 30 minutes before you plan to bake, preheat the oven to 425°F with a baking stone inside, if you have one. Place the pie pans or the parchment paper directly on the stone and spray the oven walls and floor with cold water from a spritzer bottle 3 times in the first 10 minutes. Bake for 22 to 25 minutes, or until golden. Decorate the *focacce* with the whole sage leaves and return to the oven for about 30 seconds. Remove from the oven and immediately brush the surfaces with olive oil. Transfer the *focacce* from the baking pans to racks. Serve warm or at room temperature.

❧ *Makes three 9-inch round* focacce; *serves 10 to 12*

VARIATION: To make smaller *focacce*, divide the dough into 6 equal pieces; bake for 18 to 20 minutes.

Focaccia from Puglia
FOCACCIA PUGLIESE

❀

I first ate this particular thick, soft-textured focaccia in one of a cluster of caves from the early Middle Ages near the Hotel Melograno outside Monopoli. The domed space had once been a frantoio for pressing olives into oil, but in its current incarnation it has been whitewashed and has become a startlingly beautiful dining room. Late in the evening, lanterns light the interior and dapple a buffet table full of such local specialties as this focaccia with strands of sweet red peppers that look like a mysterious edible calligraphy. Its height and light texture come from the presence of mashed potatoes in the dough.

DOUGH

8 ounces small boiling potatoes

1 ½ teaspoons active dry yeast

¼ cup warm water, 105° to 115°F

1 cup water, room temperature

1 tablespoon fruity olive oil

3 ¾ cups (500 grams) durum flour

2 ½ teaspoons sea salt

TOPPING

1 or 2 sweet red peppers

3 tablespoons extra-virgin olive oil

Sea salt

❧ About 30 minutes before you are ready to make the dough, peel the potatoes and boil them until they are tender. Drain and mash or press them through a ricer. Use the potatoes while they are still warm but not so hot as to kill the yeast; they should be about the same temperature as the warm water.

❧ Whisk the yeast into the warm water in a large mixing or mixer bowl and let stand until creamy, about 10 minutes. Stir in the room-temperature water and the olive oil. If you are making the focaccia by hand, add the mashed potatoes, salt, and 1 cup of flour at a time and mix with a wooden spoon so that the dough comes together well. Knead on a floured work surface for 10 minutes until the dough is velvety, elastic, smooth, and a bit sticky. You may need to use your dough scraper now and then to scrape away a thin film of dough that forms on the work surface.

❧ If you are using a heavy-duty electric mixer, use the paddle attachment to stir the potatoes, flour, and salt into the yeast mixture and mix for 3 minutes. Change to the dough hook and knead for 5 minutes at medium speed, or until the dough is velvety, elastic, smooth, and slightly sticky. You may want to finish kneading by hand for 1 minute on a lightly floured work surface so that the dough loses its stickiness.

❧ First rise. Place the dough in a lightly oiled container, cover it tightly with plastic wrap, and let rise until doubled, about 1¼ to 1½ hours.

❧ Topping. While the dough is rising, roast and peel the peppers. Place them on a broiler pan about 3 inches from the heat or roast them over a high gas flame until the skins are evenly blistered and charred. Move them to a paper or plastic bag, close it tightly, and allow them to rest for 15 to 30 minutes. Cut the peppers in half, remove the stems, seeds, and ribs, and peel off the skins; they should come off easily. Slice the peppers in thin strands and set them aside.

Shaping and second rise. Divide the dough in half and spread each piece to fill the bottom of a well-oiled 10-inch pie pan. Cover with towels and let rise until doubled, about 1 hour.

Baking. At least 30 minutes before you plan to bake, preheat the oven to 400°F with a baking stone inside, if you have one. Just before baking, dimple the dough with your fingertips, drizzle with olive oil, and scatter the peppers over the top so that they make a beautiful abstract design. Sprinkle with the sea salt. Place the pans directly on the baking stone, spray the oven walls and floor with cold water from a spritzer bottle 3 times in the first 10 minutes, and bake for 22 to 25 minutes, or until the tops and undersides of the *focacce* are golden. Immediately remove from the baking pans and place on a rack.

Serve warm or at room temperature.

Makes two 10-inch round focacce; *serves 8 to 10*

PUGLIESE FOCACCIA WITH TOMATOES (*FOCACCIA PUGLIESE CON POMODORI*): Use 2 peeled, seeded, and finely chopped tomatoes instead of sweet peppers. Just before baking, drizzle the top of the dough with olive oil, dapple with shreds of tomatoes, and sprinkle with coarse salt.

Schiacciata Covered with Caramelized Onions
SCHIACCIATA ALLE CIPOLLE

The longer you cook the onions over very low heat, the sweeter they become as they caramelize. Be sure not to let them brown; they will do that once they are in the oven.

DOUGH

Schiacciata with Starter dough (page 36), made through the first rise

TOPPING

2 white or red onions, finely sliced

5 to 6 tablespoons olive oil

Sea salt

Freshly ground black pepper

Shaping and second rise. After the dough has risen, divide it into 3 equal pieces and with moist hands spread each in an oiled 9-inch pie pan, or spread all the dough in an oiled 11 x 17-inch baking pan. Cover with towels and let rise again until doubled, about 2 hours.

Meanwhile, warm 3 tablespoons olive oil in a medium sauté pan or heavy skillet and cook the sliced onions over very low heat for 25 to 30 minutes, stirring every few minutes. Cover and continue cooking until the onions are sweet, caramelized, and almost melting, about 1 hour in all. Check from time to time to be sure the onions are not dry; add a little water if necessary, and be careful that they don't brown. Set aside to cool.

Third rise and topping. Dimple the dough vigorously. Drizzle it with 1 or 2 tablespoons of olive oil, arrange the onions over the top, sprinkle with salt and pepper, cover, and let stand for 30 minutes.

Baking. At least 30 minutes before you plan to bake, preheat the oven to 425°F with a baking stone inside, if you have one. Just before baking, sprinkle the dough with a bit more oil, being sure to moisten the edges. Set the pan directly on the stone and spray the oven walls and floor with cold water 3 times in the first 10 minutes. Bake for 5 minutes, reduce the temperature to 400°F, and continue baking until the dough is golden brown, 20 to 25 minutes. Remove immediately from the pan and place on a rack. Serve warm or at room temperature.

❧ *Makes three 9-inch round schiacciate or one 11 x 17-inch schiacciata; serves 10 to 12*

Schiacciata with Slices of Tomatoes and Shredded Basil

SCHIACCCIATA AI POMODORI E BASILICO

❦

H*ere's the taste of summer on a crunchy slice of flat bread. If you have tomatoes in your garden or can find some at a local farmer's market, snatch them up because they will be full of flavor from ripening on the vine. Otherwise, choose any kind of ripe and mellow toma-to to flavor your schiacciata: red, yellow, orange, even pale celadon green with darker stripes.*

DOUGH

Schiacciata with Starter dough (page 36), made through the first rise

TOPPING

Extra-virgin olive oil

2 or 3 ripe tomatoes, sliced ½ to ¾ inch thick

½ teaspoon dried oregano, or 1 handful fresh basil leaves, finely sliced

Sea salt

Freshly ground black pepper

❧ Shaping and second rise. After the dough has risen, you may divide it into 3 equal pieces and set each in a 9-inch oiled pie pan, or you may spread the entire dough in an oiled 11 x 17-inch baking pan. Cover with towels and let rise again until doubled, about 2 hours.

❧ Third rise and topping. Dimple the dough vigorously, letting your fingers pummel the surface to create deep holes. Drizzle with olive oil and arrange the tomatoes in a layer over the top. If you are using dried oregano, sprinkle it over the tomatoes along with the salt and pepper. Cover and let stand for 30 minutes.

❧ Baking. At least 30 minutes before baking, preheat the oven as directed to 425°F with a baking stone in-side, if you have one. Just before baking, drizzle a little more oil over the top and edges of the dough, making sure that it moistens both. Place the pan directly on the stone and spray the oven walls and floor with cold water from a spritzer bottle 3 times in the first 10 min-utes. Bake for 5 minutes, reduce the temperature to 400°F, and continue baking until the dough is golden brown, about 20 to 25 minutes. Remove from the oven and immediately transfer to a rack. Sprinkle fresh basil leaves, if you are using them, over the top, pressing them into the holes on the surface where possible. Serve warm or at room temperature.

❧ *Makes three 9-inch round schiacciate or one 11 x 17-inch schiacciata; serves 10 to 12*

Cornmeal Schiacciata with Walnuts

SCHIACCIATA RUSTICA CON NOCI

There's something magical about this focaccia with its combined crunch of cornmeal and toasted walnuts. Although we'll never know what enterprising person from the Tuscan hinterlands dreamed it up, we can guess that it was probably someone who peered into the larder on a cold winter day and scooped up what was left—a handful of cornmeal and a few walnuts—tossed them together, and turned an ordinary focaccia into a tantalizing country dish. Cut the focaccia into wedges and set it out in place of bread or serve it at the end of a meal with shards of Parmesan cheese and a glass of red wine.

DOUGH

2½ teaspoons (1 package) active dry yeast

1⅓ cups warm water, 105° to 115°F

2 tablespoons olive oil

½ cup plus 2 teaspoons (80 grams) cornmeal

3 cups (420 grams) unbleached all-purpose flour

1½ teaspoons sea salt

½ cup plus 2 tablespoons walnuts

TOPPING

Olive oil

Coarse sea salt

❧ Sprinkle the yeast over the warm water in a large mixing or mixer bowl, whisk it in, and let stand until creamy, about 10 minutes. Stir in the olive oil. If you are making this by hand, combine the cornmeal, flour, and salt, and whisk 1 cup into the yeast mixture. Use a wooden spoon to mix in the rest, 1 cup at a time, until a firm dough is formed. Knead on a lightly floured work surface for 8 to 10 minutes, or until firm.

❧ If you are using a heavy-duty electric mixer, add the cornmeal, flour, and salt to the yeast mixture and mix with the paddle attachment until a firm dough is formed. Change to the dough hook and knead for about 3 minutes, or until the dough is firm and slightly sticky. Knead the dough briefly on a lightly floured surface to eliminate any stickiness.

❧ First rise. Place the dough in a lightly oiled container, cover it tightly with plastic wrap, and let rise until doubled, about 45 minutes. While the dough is rising, preheat the oven to 350°F, place the walnuts in a baking pan, and toast them for 15 minutes. Set aside to cool.

❧ Shaping and second rise. Flatten the dough on a lightly floured work surface into a 7 x 14-inch rectangle. Sprinkle the walnuts over the top, leaving a 1-inch margin around the edges. Turn in the sides, roll up the dough, and flatten it gently with your palms, keeping the walnuts inside from bursting through the surface. Place in an oiled 10½ x 15½-inch baking pan and flatten and stretch the dough as far as you can toward the edges. Cover with a towel and leave for 10 minutes, then stretch the dough again until it fills the bottom of the pan. Cover with a towel and let rise until doubled, about 1 hour.

❧ Baking. At least 30 minutes before you plan to bake, preheat the oven to 400°F with a baking stone inside, if you have one. Just before baking, dimple the dough lightly with your fingertips, drizzle a light veil of olive oil over the top, and sprinkle with sea salt. Set the pan directly on the stone and bake until golden, about 20 to 25 minutes, spraying the oven walls and floor with cold water from a spritzer bottle 3 times in the first 10 minutes. Transfer the focaccia from the pan to a rack. Serve warm or at room temperature.

❧ *Makes one 10½ x 15½-inch focaccia; serves 8 to 10*

VARIATION: CORNMEAL SCHIACCIATA WITH HAZELNUTS (*SCHIACCIATA ALLE NOCCIOLE*): Use toasted and skinned hazelnuts in place of the walnuts. Heat the oven to 350°F. Toast the hazelnuts on a baking sheet until the skins blister, 10 to 15 minutes. Wrap them in a kitchen towel and let stand 10 to 15 minutes, then rub the skins off with the towel.

Schiacciata with Ribbons of Sweet Peppers
SCHIACCIATA AI PEPERONI

❦

DOUGH
Schiacciata with Starter dough (page 36), made through the first rise

TOPPING
2 to 3 sweet yellow and red peppers
Olive oil
Coarse sea salt

GARNISH
Finely sliced fresh basil leaves, finely chopped flat-leaf parsley, or a handful of rinsed and drained capers

❧ Shaping and second rise. After the dough has risen once, spread it with moist hands in an oiled 11 x 17-inch baking pan. Cover with towels and let rise again until doubled, about 2 hours.

❧ While the dough is rising, roast and peel the peppers. To do so, either place them on a broiler pan and broil them about 3 inches from the heat or roast them over a high gas flame until the skins are evenly blistered and charred. Transfer them to a paper or plastic bag, close it tightly, and set aside for 15 to 30 minutes. When the peppers are cool enough to handle, cut them in half, remove the stems, ribs, and seeds, and peel off the skins. Cut the peppers into ½-inch ribbons.

❧ Third rise and topping. Dimple the dough vigorously, letting your fingers create little holes in the dough where the oil can pool. Drizzle with olive oil, scatter the strips of peppers over the surface, and sprinkle with sea salt. Cover and let stand for 30 minutes.

❧ Baking. At least 30 minutes before you plan to bake, preheat the oven to 425°F with a baking stone inside, if you have one. Just before baking, drizzle a bit more oil over the top of the dough. Don't be sparing; it is important that both peppers and dough be moistened with oil. Sprinkle with the basil or parsley or press a handful of capers into the dough. Place the baking pan directly on the stone, spraying the oven walls and floor with cold water from a spritzer bottle 3 times in the first 10 minutes. Bake for 5 minutes, then reduce the temperature to 400°F and continue baking until the dough is golden brown, about 20 to 25 minutes.

❧ Immediately transfer the pan to a rack. Serve warm or at room temperature.

❧ *Makes one 11 x 17-inch* schiacciata; *serves 10 to 12*

Focaccia with Sun-dried Tomatoes

FOCACCIA AI POMODORI SECCHI

❦

This recipe works wonderfully well when made in a mixer because the sun-dried tomatoes marble the dough in a beautiful pattern. If you decide to make it by hand, first puree the sun-dried tomatoes in a food processor or blender.

DOUGH

2 teaspoons active dry yeast

¼ cup warm water, 105° to 115°F

1¾ cups plus 1 tablespoon water, room temperature

2 tablespoons olive oil, preferably from the sun-dried tomatoes

12 to 16 sun-dried tomatoes packed in oil, drained

5¼ cups (740 grams) unbleached all-purpose flour, plus 2 or 3 tablespoons, as needed

2¼ teaspoons sea salt

TOPPING

Olive oil

6 to 8 sun-dried tomatoes, drained and slivered

Fresh basil leaves (optional)

❧ Sprinkle the yeast over the warm water in a large mixing or mixer bowl, whisk it in, and let stand until creamy, about 10 minutes. Stir the room-temperature water and the reserved oil into the yeast mixture. If you are making the dough by hand, puree the tomatoes in a blender or food processor and add them to the yeast mixture. Mix in the 5¼ cups flour and the salt in 3 additions. Turn the dough out onto a lightly floured work surface and, using the 2 to 3 tablespoons of flour, knead for 7 to 10 minutes, with a brief rest halfway through, or until the dough is velvety and elastic.

❧ If you are using a heavy-duty mixer, add the flour, salt, and tomatoes to the yeast mixture and mix with the paddle attachment until the dough comes together. Change to the dough hook and knead for 2 minutes on low, then 2 minutes on medium speed, or until the dough easily clears the sides of the bowl and is velvety and elastic.

❧ First rise. Place the dough in a lightly oiled container, cover it tightly with plastic wrap, and let rise until doubled, about 1 hour.

❧ Shaping and second rise. Divide the dough into 2 pieces, one twice as large as the other. Place the smaller one in a well-oiled 10-inch pie pan and the larger into a well-oiled 10½ x 15½-inch baking pan. Stretch the dough outward to reach the edges of each pan. Dimple lightly with your fingertips, drizzle oil over the top, cover with a towel, and let rise until doubled, about 1 hour.

❧ Baking. Thirty minutes before you are ready to bake, preheat the oven to 400°F with a baking stone inside, if you have one. Arrange the slivered sun-dried tomatoes over the tops of the *focacce*, sprinkle with a little more oil if the dough seems a bit dry, and place the large focaccia in the oven directly on the preheated stone and set the smaller one on an oven rack. Spray the oven walls and floor with cold water from a spritzer bottle 3 times in the first 10 minutes and bake for 20 to 25 minutes, or until golden. Remove the *focacce* from the oven and immediately spread the optional basil leaves over the top. Let the *focacce* cool in their pans for 2 to 3 minutes, then remove them and blot

briefly on paper towels if the bottoms seem oily. Transfer to a rack. Serve warm or at room temperature.

❧ *Makes one 10-inch round and one 10½ x 15½-inch focacce; serves 12 to 16*

Schiacciata Studded with Pancetta
SCHIACCIATA CON PANCETTA

❀

I don't know which I like more: this full-flavored chewy schiacciata all by itself with just olive oil and coarse salt on top or with the wonderful addition of pancetta, whose clove-and-cracked-pepper flavor impregnates the dough. The recipe comes from a tiny, well-hidden bakery just beyond Poggio a Caiano in Tuscany, where the young baker has replaced his grandmother, who died at 101. He continues to make this irresistible focaccia in the family's 150-year-old wood-burning oven. No wonder it sells out early in the day! It has the delicious chewiness and porous open structure of really good rustic bread, with added flavor from a topping of chunks of the meatiest type of pancetta available. Because the dough is so wet and uses a large amount of starter, it is best made in the mixer. Please remember to weigh the starter if possible; otherwise use it cold directly from the refrigerator.

DOUGH

½ teaspoon active dry yeast

⅓ cup warm water, 105° to 115°F

1 cup plus 1 tablespoon water, room temperature

2 cups (500 grams) Starter for Focaccia (page 36), 10 to 24 hours old

2 cups plus 2 tablespoons (300 grams) unbleached all-purpose flour

¾ cup (100 grams) whole-wheat flour

1½ teaspoons sea salt

TOPPING

Olive oil

Coarse sea salt

2 to 3 ounces pancetta, cubed

❧ Sprinkle the yeast over the warm water in a large mixer bowl, whisk it in, and let stand until creamy, about 10 minutes. Pour the room-temperature water into the yeast mixture, add the starter by chopping it up or squeezing it through your fingers, and mix with the paddle until the starter breaks down and the water is chalky white. Add the flours and salt and blend well, but do not expect the dough to come away from the sides of the bowl. Change to the dough hook and knead for 2 minutes on low and 2 minutes on medium speed. The dough will be sticky, but if you wet your hands and keep a bowl of water nearby, you can handle it with wet fingers. Sprinkle 1 or 2 tablespoons of flour on a work surface and knead the dough briefly until it is soft and tender.

❧ First rise. Place the dough in an oiled container, cover it tightly with plastic wrap, and let rise until doubled, about 1 hour and 30 to 45 minutes.

❧ Shaping and second rise. The dough is very sticky, but if you spread a little flour on your work surface and have a bowl of water nearby with which you can wet your hands well, you will be able to handle it. Place the dough on your lightly floured work surface. Cut off an 8-ounce piece—about 1 cup—and place it in an oiled 8-inch pie pan. Move the rest to an oiled 11 x 17-inch baking pan. The dough will resist being pressed out to the edges, so cover it with a towel and allow it to rest for 20 minutes, then press it out until it fills the bottom of the pan. Cover the dough again with the towel and let it rise only until it shows obvious bubbles and some stretch marks, about 45 minutes.

❧ Baking. Thirty minutes before you plan to bake, preheat the oven to 425°F with a baking stone inside, if you have one. Dimple the dough firmly with your moistened knuckles or thumbs (fingertips don't make much of an impression on this bubbly, still sticky dough), drizzle with threads of oil, sprinkle with salt, and press cubes of pancetta into the top. Place the pans directly on the preheated stone—you may need to put the round pie pan on a separate rack—and spray the oven walls and floor with cold water from a spritzer bottle 3 times in the first 10 minutes. Bake for about 25 minutes, or until golden. Slide the *focacce* out of the pans immediately and let cool slightly on a rack so that the bottom crusts don't get soggy. Serve warm or at room temperature.

❧ *Makes one 11 x 17-inch and one 8-inch round focaccia; serves 10 to 14*

Gorgonzola, Red Onion, and Walnut Focaccia
FOCACCIA AL GORGONZOLA

This delicious dough comes directly from the Lunigiana area at the southernmost part of Liguria, but the topping is my fantasia, an irresistible combination that is equally at home as part of a meal or as dessert with fresh figs. Be sure to use the mellow Dolcelatte type of Gorgonzola cheese, so that its creaminess can play off against the crunch of the walnuts and the sweetness of red onions.

DOUGH
½ cup milk, warmed to 105° to 115°F
2½ teaspoons (1 package) active dry yeast
1 cup water, room temperature
1½ tablespoons extra-virgin olive oil or best-quality lard
3¾ cups (500 grams) unbleached all-purpose flour
2½ teaspoons sea salt

TOPPING
¾ cup walnuts
1 red onion
8 ounces Gorgonzola cheese, Dolcelatte variety
1½ to 2 tablespoons milk
Olive oil

❧ Place the warmed milk in a mixing or mixer bowl, sprinkle the yeast over the top, and whisk it in; let stand until creamy, about 10 minutes. Stir in the room-temperature water and olive oil or lard. If you are making this dough by hand, mix the flour and salt together and stir in, 1 cup at a time, mixing well with a wooden

spoon until a dough is formed. Knead on a lightly floured work surface for 6 to 8 minutes, or until the dough is smooth and elastic.

❧ If you are using a heavy-duty electric mixer, add the flour and salt to the yeast mixture with the paddle attachment and mix until a dough is formed. Change to the dough hook and knead for 3 minutes, or until the dough is smooth, elastic, and slightly sticky.

❧ First rise. Transfer the dough to a lightly oiled container, cover tightly with plastic wrap, and let rise until doubled, about 1 hour. The dough should be fluffy but still sticky and full of air bubbles.

❧ Topping. While the dough is rising, toast the walnuts in a preheated 350°F oven for 10 to 15 minutes. Set aside to cool. Cut the onion into quarters and place in boiling water to cover for 1 to 2 minutes. Drain, pat dry with a towel, let cool briefly, and slice finely. Whirl the Gorgonzola and milk together in a blender or food processor to make a creamy spread. Transfer to a medium bowl and stir in the walnuts and onion slices with a rubber spatula.

❧ Shaping. If you choose to make 1 flat focaccia, move the dough to an oiled 10½ x 15½-inch pan. Otherwise, divide the dough into 3 equal parts and place each in an oiled 8- or 9-inch pie pan. Stretch and press the dough out toward the edges until it resists, cover it with towels, and let it relax for 10 minutes. Then press the dough out again until it covers the bottom and reaches the edges of the pans. Spread the cheese mixture evenly over the dough with a rubber spatula or wooden spoon.

❧ Second rise. Drizzle a little olive oil over the edges of the dough and let rise until well puffed, about 1 hour.

❧ Baking. Thirty minutes before you are ready to bake, preheat the oven to 400°F with a baking stone inside, if you have one. Place the pan or pans directly on the stone and bake for 10 minutes, spraying the oven walls and floor with cold water from a spritzer bottle 3 times. Reduce the heat to 375°F and bake until the topping is golden brown, about 10 minutes, taking care that the cheese doesn't burn. Remove from the pan or pans and serve the focaccia while it is still hot, although it is also delicious at a warm room temperature.

❧ *Makes one 10½ x 15½-inch focaccia or three 8- or 9-inch round focacce; serves 10 to 12*

Focaccia with Olive Oil and White Wine
FOCACCIA IMPASTATA AL'OLIO

❀

This delicious focaccia comes straight from the book La cuciniera genovese by Giambattista and Giovanni Ratto, a mid-nineteenth-century collection of recipes from Genoa that is now in its eighteenth edition. I have not changed any directions for timing or amounts of ingredients and am amazed that we can follow them easily at this distance in time and space. When Ratti father and son write that one rise will take 3 hours in the summer and 5 in the winter, their instructions still hold true today. There is no yeast in the recipe beyond what is in the starter; this may account for the firm, chewy texture of the focaccia. It must not rise higher than ½ to ¾ inch. Please let the heavy-duty mixer handle this very wet dough.

DOUGH

2¾ cups water, cool room temperature in summer, warmer
    in winter

Scant ½ cup (110 grams) Starter for Focaccia (page 36),
    8 to 10 hours old

7½ cups (1000 grams) unbleached all-purpose flour

2½ tablespoons plus 1 teaspoon extra-virgin olive oil,
    preferably from Liguria

⅓ cup dry white wine

2½ teaspoons sea salt

TOPPING

About 4 tablespoons extra-virgin olive oil

About 1½ to 2 teaspoons coarse sea salt

❧ Place the water in a large mixer bowl and chop up or squeeze the starter into it through your fingers. Use the paddle to stir in the flour and beat well; change to the dough hook and knead for 3 to 4 minutes, or until the dough is stiff, elastic, and slightly sticky.

❧ First rise. Transfer the dough to a lightly oiled container, cover it tightly with plastic wrap, and let rise until doubled, about 4 hours.

❧ Second rise. Return the dough to the mixer bowl, but do not use the mixer at this point because liquid will fly everywhere. Beat in the olive oil by hand a bit at a time, then add the wine with the salt dissolved in it. Once you have stirred these together, you can set the dough hook in place and use the mixer to knead, for 3 to 4 minutes, what will become a very sticky dough that seems as moist as a starter. Move the dough to a lightly oiled container, cover it with plastic wrap, and let rise until doubled, about 3 hours if the weather and your kitchen are warm or 5 if chilly and wintry. The dough will have big air bubbles; it will be very jiggly in texture and extremely sticky but elastic.

❧ Shaping. Turn the dough out onto a lightly floured work surface and divide it in half. Please resist the impulse to use lots of flour. Sprinkle tiny amounts of flour on top just to counteract the stickiness. Place each piece of dough on a well-oiled 10½ x 15½-inch baking pan. The dough will be sticky, soft, and resistant, so wet your hands and press it out as much as you can; let it rest for 2 or 3 minutes before pressing some more to stretch it toward the edges. Cover the pans with very wet towels and let the dough rise for 45 minutes; you will need to wet the towels again after 20 minutes. Stretch the dough again, dimple the sticky surface forcefully with your thumb or knuckles (fingertips simply won't make enough of an impression), drizzle with oil, and sprinkle coarse salt over the top.

❧ Baking. Thirty minutes before you plan to bake, preheat the oven to 425°F with a baking stone inside, if you have one. Bake 1 pan of dough at a time and cover and set the other one aside. Place the pan directly on the preheated stone and spray the oven walls and floor with cold water from a spritzer bottle 3 times during the first 10 minutes. Bake the focaccia until golden, 30 to 35 minutes. Repeat with the second focaccia. Remove each from the pan immediately and place on a rack. Serve warm or at room temperature.

❧ Makes two 10½ x 15½-focacce; serves 12 to 16

VARIATION: Mix 20 to 25 fresh sage leaves into the dough. Just before taking the focacce out of the oven, arrange a few sage leaves on top for decoration.

Schiacciata with Slivers of Potatoes and Rosemary

SCHIACCIATA ALLE PATATE E ROSMARINO

❀

The first time I saw a schiacciata paved with potatoes, I thought I would be overwhelmed by carbohydrates, but that was before I actually tasted this delicious combination. Carlo Sarti, the Florentine baker who gave me his recipe, fills the cases and shelves of his bakery with schiacciate of many grains and flavorings, but this group of recipes — see the schiacciate with onions, tomatoes, and sweet red peppers — is the one I always come back to.

DOUGH

Schiacciata with Starter dough (page 36), made through the first rise

TOPPING

Extra-virgin olive oil

8 ounces new potatoes

1 tablespoon minced fresh rosemary

Sea salt

Freshly ground black pepper

❧ Shaping and second rise. After the dough has risen once, divide it into 3 equal pieces and with moist hands spread each in an oiled 9-inch pie pan, or spread all the dough in an oiled 11 x 17-inch baking pan. Cover with towels and let rise again until doubled, about 2 hours.

❧ While the dough is rising, boil the potatoes for 8 to 10 minutes, or until a knife can just pierce their interiors easily. Let cool to room temperature and cut into thin slices.

❧ Third rise and topping. Dimple the dough with vigor; you can really let your fingers dance over the top because the dough is extremely responsive. Drizzle with olive oil and arrange the potatoes in a single layer over the top. Sprinkle with the rosemary, salt, and pepper, cover, and let rise for 30 minutes.

❧ Baking. At least 30 minutes before you plan to bake, preheat the oven to 425°F with a baking stone inside, if you have one. Just before baking, drizzle more oil over the top of the *schiacciata*. Don't be sparing at this moment; the oil should moisten the potatoes as well as the edges of the dough. Place the pan directly on the stone and spray the oven walls and floor with cold water 3 times in the first 10 minutes. Bake for 5 minutes, reduce the temperature to 400°F, and continue baking until the dough is golden brown although the potatoes remain pale, about 20 to 25 minutes. Immediately transfer from the baking pan to a rack. Serve warm or at room temperature.

❧ *Makes three 9-inch round schiacciate or one 11 x 17-inch schiacciata; serves 10 to 12*

Sweet Pepper Focaccia from Majorca

COCA DE PREBES TORRATS

❀

It may not be surprising that pizza and focaccia turn up in Majorca, the Spanish island in the Mediterranean —after all, the Romans were there two millenia ago. Paula Wolfert, the well-known expert on Mediterranean food, sent me the recipe, which she, in turn, got from Colman Andrews, an authority on Catalan cooking. The recipe was originally for pizza, and I changed it only slightly to turn it into a focaccia that can be made in one hour from beginning to end.

TOPPING

3 to 4 large sweet red peppers

2 tablespoons olive oil

6 cloves garlic, minced

2 tablespoons finely chopped fresh flat-leaf parsley

Sea salt

DOUGH

1 tablespoon active dry yeast

1 cup minus 1 tablespoon (15 tablespoons) warm water, 105° to 115°F

1½ tablespoons good-quality olive oil

1 teaspoon best-quality lard (optional)

2 cups (280 grams) unbleached all-purpose flour

¾ teaspoon sea salt

❧ Begin by roasting the peppers for the topping. Set them on a broiler pan and broil about 3 inches from the heat or roast over a high gas flame until the skins are evenly blistered and charred. Place them in a paper or plastic bag, close it tightly, and let them rest for 15 to 30 minutes. Meanwhile, heat the 2 tablespoons of olive oil in a small sauté pan or heavy skillet, and sauté the garlic over low heat for 2 or 3 minutes, being careful not to let it burn. Set aside to cool slightly. Cut the peppers in half, remove the stems, ribs, and seeds, and peel off the skins. Slice the peppers into thin strips.

❧ Sprinkle the yeast over the warm water in a medium bowl, whisk it in, and let stand until creamy, about 10 minutes. Stir in 1½ tablespoons of the oil and the optional lard. If you are making this by hand, combine the flour and salt and stir them in, 1 cup at a time, with a wooden spoon until the dough comes together. Knead on a lightly floured work surface until the dough is soft, smooth, and elastic, about 5 minutes.

❧ If you are using a heavy-duty mixer, set the paddle attachment in place, add the flour and salt to the yeast mixture, and mix until the dough comes together. Change to the dough hook and knead for 2 to 3 minutes, or until the dough is smooth, soft, and elastic.

❧ First rise. Shape the dough into a ball, place in an lightly oiled container, cover tightly with plastic wrap, and let rise for 20 minutes.

❧ At least 30 minutes before you are planning to bake, heat the oven to 400°F with a baking stone inside, if you have one.

❧ Shaping and second rise. Move the risen dough to an oiled 9-inch square baking pan. The dough will be supple and stretch easily to fit the bottom of the pan. Dimple it with your fingertips, drizzle with the garlic-infused oil, and scatter the pepper strips and parsley over the top; sprinkle with salt. Cover with a towel and let rise for another 20 minutes.

❧ Baking. Set the pan directly on the heated stone and bake until the focaccia is golden, about 25 minutes. Cool briefly, then remove from the pan and place on a rack. Serve warm or at room temperature.

Makes one 9-inch square focaccia; serves 6 to 8

Focaccia with White Whole-Wheat Flour
FOCACCIA DI FARINA DI GRANO BIANCO

❀

What makes this nutty-tasting focaccia different from others? One thing only: It is made with white whole-wheat, a new strain that is different from the wheat from which most flour is milled. This sweet wheat with its golden flecks looks almost as light as all-purpose flour but has the nutritiousness of whole wheat. Please see the Source List (page 112) for where to find it.

You must make the starter at least 12 hours before you make the dough. Because of the stickiness of the starter and the dough, this focaccia is more easily done with the electric mixer. If you decide to brave the process by hand, be sure to have some extra flour nearby, but use it as sparingly as possible to avoid changing the nature of the dough.

DOUGH

2½ teaspoons (1 package) active dry yeast

½ cup warm water, 105° to 115°F

¾ cup plus 2 tablespoons (200 grams) Starter for Focaccia (page 36), at least 12 hours old

2½ cups water, room temperature

7½ cups (1000 grams) white whole-wheat flour

1 tablespoon sea salt

TOPPING

6 tablespoons extra-virgin olive oil

2 sweet red peppers, roasted, ribs and seeds removed, peeled, and sliced into ribbons (previous page)

¾ teaspoon coarse sea salt

A few fresh oregano sprigs, or ½ to ¾ teaspoon dried oregano

❧ Sprinkle the yeast over the warm water in a large mixing or mixer bowl; whisk it in and let stand until creamy, about 5 to 10 minutes. Chop up the starter; mix it and the room-temperature water into the yeast mixture. If you are making the dough by hand, combine the flour and salt and mix them in, 1 cup at a time, with a wooden spoon until the dough is well blended. Turn it out onto a floured work surface. Knead for 6 to 8 minutes, or until bubbles develop under the surface. The dough will become sticky as you knead; keep some extra flour nearby, using it as sparingly as possible.

❧ If you are using a heavy-duty electric mixer, set the paddle attachment in place, add the flour and salt to the yeast mixture, and stir until a dough is formed, 3 to 4 minutes; the dough will pull away from the sides but not the bottom of the mixer bowl. Change to the dough hook and knead at medium speed until the dough is elastic, sticky, and soft but not wet, about 5 minutes. You will see many bubbles under the skin.

❧ First rise. Place the dough in a lightly oiled container, cover it tightly with plastic wrap, and let rise until doubled, about 1 hour.

❧ Shaping and second rise. Prepare two 10½ x 15½-inch baking pans by pouring 2½ tablespoons of olive oil into each, then tilting to cover the bottom and sides well. Turn the elastic, slightly sticky dough out onto a lightly floured work surface, cut it in half, and sprinkle it very lightly with just enough flour to counteract the stickiness. Place each piece in a prepared baking pan and flatten and stretch the dough to cover as much of the bottom as possible. Cover with a towel and let the dough relax for 10 minutes, then stretch the dough toward the edges again, cover, and let rise until puffy, 45 minutes to 1 hour.

❧ Topping. Dimple the tops vigorously with your index fingers and brush them with the remaining 1 tablespoon of oil as well as some of the excess oil made available by tilting the pan and siphoning it from the bottom. Sprinkle the dough with the pieces of sweet pepper, crystals of coarse salt, and a little oregano, and finish by drizzling with a little more oil.

❧ Baking. At least 30 minutes before you plan to bake, preheat the oven to 425°F with a baking stone inside, if you have one. Bake one focaccia first; cover the second and set it aside. Set the baking pan directly on the preheated stone and reduce the heat to 400°F, spraying the oven walls and floor with cold water from a spritzer bottle 3 times in the first 10 minutes. Bake until the focaccia is golden, 18 to 20 minutes. Immediately remove the focaccia from the baking pan and place on paper towels to absorb any excess oil. Cool to a warm room temperature on a rack. Repeat with the second focaccia.

Makes two 10½ x 15½-inch focacce; serves 12 to 16

Focaccia Covered with Leeks
FOCACCIA AI PORRI

❧

As surprising as it may seem, many Italians would immediately know that this focaccia comes from Puglia, where potatoes grow with abandon and find their way into numerous dishes. The potatoes give it surprising height—2 inches—and an interior honeycombed with pores. But there are other secrets: The dough gets some lovely color from the milk, while the starter and egg give it a bit of keeping power. It is best to weigh your starter, since it expands at room temperature, but if you don't have a scale, scoop it cold from the refrigerator. The caramelized leeks are a delicious topping, but be careful to keep them from browning while they cook; the oven will take care of that later. You may substitute unbleached all-purpose flour for the golden durum flour, although the focaccia won't taste quite as rich or deeply wheaty.

DOUGH

8 ounces boiling potatoes

1½ teaspoons active dry yeast

1 cup milk, warmed to 105° to 115°F

¼ cup water, room temperature

1 tablespoon olive oil

1 egg, room temperature, lightly beaten

1 heaping cup (250 grams) Starter for Focaccia (page 36)

3¾ cups (500 grams) durum flour, plus 1 or 2 tablespoons
　　as needed

2½ teaspoons sea salt

5 *tablespoons olive oil*
9 *leeks (about 2 pounds), cleaned very well and thinly*
    sliced; use white parts only
¾ *teaspoon sea salt*

❧ About 30 minutes before you are ready to make the dough, peel the potatoes and boil them until they are tender; drain and mash or press them through a ricer. Use the potatoes while they are still warm but not so hot as to kill the yeast; they should be about the same temperature as the milk.

❧ Sprinkle the yeast over the warm milk in a large mixing or mixer bowl and whisk it in; let stand until creamy, about 10 minutes. Stir in the water, olive oil, and egg. Chop up or squeeze the starter through your fingers into the bowl and mix well. If you are making the focaccia by hand, use a wooden spoon to stir in the mashed potatoes, then add the 3¾ cups flour and the salt in 2 additions and mix well so that the dough comes together. Knead on a lightly floured work surface for 10 minutes, or until the dough is velvety, elastic, and smooth but slightly sticky. You may want to use 1 to 2 tablespoons of flour to counteract the stickiness.

❧ If you are making the dough with a heavy-duty electric mixer, stir in the potatoes, 3¾ cups of flour, and salt into the yeast mixture with the paddle attachment and mix for 3 minutes. Change to the dough hook and knead for 5 minutes at medium speed, or until the dough is velvety, elastic, smooth, and slightly sticky. You may knead the dough by hand for 1 minute on a lightly floured work surface with 1 to 2 tablespoons of flour, if necessary, so that it loses its stickiness.

❧ First rise. Place the dough in a lightly oiled container, cover tightly with plastic wrap, and let rise until doubled, about 1¼ to 1½ hours.

❧ Topping. While the dough is rising, heat 3 tablespoons of the olive oil in a large sauté pan or heavy skillet, add the sliced leeks, and cook over the lowest possible heat for about 20 minutes, stirring occasionally and being very careful not to let the leeks brown. Cover and check frequently in the next 10 minutes to be sure they cook slowly; add a little water if they are getting dry. Set aside to cool.

❧ Shaping and second rise. Divide the dough in half and flatten and stretch each piece to cover the bottom of a well-oiled 10-inch round pie pan. Cover with a damp towel and let rise until doubled, about 1 hour.

❧ Baking. At least 30 minutes before you plan to bake, preheat the oven to 400°F with a baking stone inside, if you have one. Just before baking, dimple the tops of the dough with your fingertips. Drizzle with the remaining olive oil, spread the leeks over the top, and sprinkle with the salt. Set the pie pans directly on the heated stone and spray the oven walls and floor with cold water from a spritzer bottle 3 times in the first 10 minutes. Bake until the tops of the *focacce* are golden, 22 to 25 minutes. Slide the *focacce* out of their pans immediately and blot them on paper towels if the bottoms seem oily. Transfer to a rack. Serve warm or at room temperature.

❧ *Makes two 10-inch round* focacce; *serves 8 to 10*

Spelt Flour Focaccia
FOCACCIA DI SPELTA

E*ven more remarkable than the flavor of this focaccia is the fact that some people who are normally sensitive to wheat can eat spelt, an ancient form of wheat with very high gluten. Spelt is easily digested because it dissolves readily in water. While it looks a bit like whole-wheat flour in color, spelt has a nutty flavor and produces a slightly chewy texture. It makes an unexpectedly delicious focaccia.*

The starter, also made of white spelt flour, must be made at least 12 hours before you make the dough, although it is at its tastiest after 3 days. Because of the stickiness of the starter and the dough, this focaccia is more easily made with the electric mixer. If you decide to make it by hand, be sure to have some extra flour nearby, although you must use it as sparingly as possible to avoid changing the nature of the dough. Since the starter recipe makes 3½ cups, you may want to freeze the portion you don't use.

SPELT FLOUR STARTER *(Biga di spelta)*
½ teaspoon active dry yeast
¼ cup warm water, 105° to 115°F
1½ cups water, room temperature
3¼ cups (450 grams) white spelt flour

DOUGH
2½ teaspoons (1 package) active dry yeast
½ cup warm water, 105° to 115°F
¾ cup plus 2 tablespoons (200 grams) spelt flour starter, above, at least 12 hours old
2½ cups water, room temperature
6¾ cups plus 2 tablespoons (960 grams) white spelt flour
1 tablespoon sea salt

FOR THE PANS AND TOPPING
6 tablespoons extra-virgin olive oil
1 large full-flavored ripe tomato, peeled and diced
¾ teaspoon coarse sea salt
A few fresh oregano sprigs, or ½ to ¾ teaspoon dried oregano

❧ Prepare the spelt flour starter by sprinkling the yeast over the warm water in a large mixing or mixer bowl; whisk it in and let stand until creamy, about 10 minutes. Stir in the room-temperature water and then the flour, mixing with a wooden spoon for about 2 minutes or with the paddle attachment of a heavy-duty mixer for 1 to 2 minutes.

❧ Rising. Transfer the starter to a lightly oiled bowl, cover with plastic wrap, and let rise at a cool room temperature for 6 to 24 hours. The starter will triple in volume and then collapse upon itself. It will still be wet and sticky when ready to use. Cover and set aside at room temperature for at least 12 hours. Refrigerate after 24 hours. If at all possible, weigh the starter if you measure it at room temperature.

❧ When you are ready to make the dough, sprinkle the yeast over the warm water in a large mixing or mixer bowl; whisk it in and let stand until creamy, about 10 minutes. Chop up the starter or squeeze it through your fingers and add it with the 2½ cups room-temperature water to the yeast mixture; mix with a wooden spoon until well blended. If you are making this by hand, combine the flour and salt and add them, 1 cup at a time, mixing with a wooden spoon until a dough is formed. Be prepared for the fact that the dough will become sticky as you knead; keep some extra flour nearby, using it as sparingly as possible, and knead the dough for about 4 to 5 minutes, or until bubbles develop under the surface.

❧ If you are using a heavy-duty electric mixer, add the flour and salt to the yeast mixture and mix with the paddle attachment until a dough is formed, 3 to 4 minutes. The dough will pull away from the sides of the mixer bowl but not the bottom. Change to the dough hook and knead at medium speed for 2 to 3 minutes, or until the dough is elastic, sticky, and soft but not wet. You will see many bubbles under the skin.

❧ First rise. Place the dough in a lightly oiled container, cover it tightly with plastic wrap, and let rise until doubled, about 1 hour.

❧ Shaping and second rise. Prepare two 10½ x 15½-inch baking pans by pouring 2½ tablespoons of the olive oil into each and then tilting to cover the bottom and sides well. Turn the sticky, elastic dough out onto a lightly floured work surface, divide it in half, and sprinkle the tops very lightly with just enough flour to counteract the stickiness. Place each piece in a prepared baking pan and stretch the dough outward to cover as much of the bottom as possible. It will resist, so cover it with a towel and leave it to relax for 10 minutes.

Stretch the dough more, cover, and let rise until well puffed, about 45 minutes to 1 hour.

❧ Topping. Dimple the tops vigorously with your index fingers and brush with oil, using the remaining 1 tablespoon of oil, as well as some of the excess oil made available by tilting the pan and siphoning it from the bottom. Sprinkle the dough with the pieces of tomato, crystals of coarse salt, and a little oregano, and finish by drizzling a little more oil to collect in pools on top of the dough.

❧ Baking. At least 30 minutes before you plan to bake, preheat the oven to 425°F with a baking stone inside, if you have one. Bake 1 focaccia first; cover the second and set it aside. Place the baking pan directly on the preheated stone and reduce the heat to 400°F, spraying the oven walls and floor with cold water from a spritzer bottle 3 times in the first 10 minutes. Bake until the focaccia is golden, 20 to 25 minutes. Immediately slide the focaccia out of the pan and place on paper towels to absorb any excess oil. Cool on a rack to room temperature. Repeat with the second focaccia.

❧ *Makes two 10½ x 15½-inch focacce; serves 12 to 16*

FOCACCIA WITH A COMBINATION OF WHITE AND WHOLE-WHEAT SPELT FLOURS (*FOCACCIA DI SPELTA E SPELTA INTEGRALE*): Use 3 cups minus 1 tablespoon (400 grams) white spelt flour and 4 cups (560 grams) whole-wheat spelt flour in place of all the white spelt flour in the dough.

Spelt and Durum Flour Focaccia of Maddellena Carella Sada

FOCACCIA DI FARRO O SPELTA

E GRANO DURO

❀

I first tasted this moist tomato-dappled focaccia when Maddalena Carella Sada served it to me at her apartment in Bari. Instantly captivated, I had to know what gave it its phenomenal flavor and texture. Her secret was a combination of durum and emmer (farro in Italian) flours, two grains indigenous to Puglia, the beautiful region on the heel of the Italian boot. Golden durum flour and emmer, the grains that grow across the wide Tavoliere plain, are available here and now spelt, which is reminiscent of emmer in taste, has arrived as well. (Please see the Source List on page 112.)

The starter must be made at least 12 hours before you make the dough, although it is delicious 1 or 2 days later. Because of the stickiness of the starter and the dough, this focaccia is much more easily made in the electric mixer. If you decide to attempt it by hand, be sure to have some extra flour nearby, but use it as sparingly as possible to avoid changing the nature of the dough.

2½ teaspoons (1 package) active dry yeast

½ cup warm water, 105° to 115°F

¾ cup plus 2 tablespoons (200 grams) Starter for Focaccia (page 36), at least 12 hours old

2½ cups water, room temperature

3¾ cups (500 grams) white spelt or farro flour

3¾ cups (500 grams) durum flour

1 tablespoon sea salt

FOR THE TOPPING AND PANS

10 to 11 tablespoons extra-virgin olive oil

1 large full-flavored ripe tomato, peeled and diced

¾ teaspoon coarse sea salt

A few sprigs of fresh oregano, or ½ to ¾ teaspoon dried oregano

4 garlic cloves, slivered

2 to 3 teaspoons capers, rinsed well (optional)

❧ Sprinkle the yeast over the warm water in a large mixing or mixer bowl; whisk it in and let stand until creamy, about 10 minutes. Chop up the starter or squeeze it through your fingers and add it to the bowl with the room-temperature water. If you are making the dough by hand, combine the flours and salt and use a wooden spoon to stir them into the yeast mixture, 1 cup at a time; mix until the dough comes together, which may take as long as 15 minutes. Turn the dough out onto a lightly floured work surface. Be prepared that the dough will get sticky as you knead, so keep some extra flour nearby, using it as sparingly as possible. Knead for 4 to 5 minutes, or until bubbles develop under the surface.

❧ If you are making the dough in a heavy-duty electric mixer, use the paddle attachment to mix the flours and salt into the yeast mixture until well blended, 3 to 4 minutes; the dough will pull away from the sides but not the bottom of the mixer bowl. Change to the dough hook and knead at medium speed for 2 to 3 minutes until the dough is elastic, sticky, and soft but not wet. You should see many bubbles under the skin.

❧ First rise. Place the dough in a lightly oiled container, cover it tightly with plastic wrap, and let rise until doubled, about 1 to 1¼ hours.

❧ Shaping and second rise. Prepare two 10½ x 15½-inch baking pans by pouring 2½ tablespoons of the olive oil into each, then tilting them to cover the bottom and sides well. Turn the elastic, quite sticky dough out onto a lightly floured work surface, cut it in half, and sprinkle it very lightly with flour, just enough to counteract the stickiness. Place each piece in a prepared baking pan and flatten and stretch the dough to cover as much of the bottom as possible. The dough will resist, so cover it with a towel and let it relax for 10 minutes. Stretch the dough some more, cover, and let rise until well puffed, 45 minutes to 1 hour.

❧ Topping. Dance your fingertips across the tops of the dough to dimple them vigorously and brush each with 2½ tablespoons of the remaining oil, using some of the excess oil available by tilting the pan and siphoning it from the bottom. Sprinkle with the pieces of tomato, crystals of coarse salt, and a little oregano, and press the garlic slivers and optional capers into the dough. Finish by drizzling with a little more oil.

❧ Baking. At least 30 minutes before you plan to bake, preheat the oven to 425°F with a baking stone inside, if you have one. Work with one focaccia at a time; cover and set the other one aside. Place the baking pan directly on the preheated stone and reduce the heat to 400°F, spraying the oven walls and floor with cold water from a spritzer bottle 3 times in the first 10 minutes. Bake until the focaccia is golden, 18 to 20 minutes. Immediately remove from the pan and blot the bottom on paper towels. Cool on a rack to warm room temperature. Repeat with the second focaccia.

❧ *Makes two 10½ x 15½-inch* focacce; *serves 12 to 16*

FILLED AND DOUBLE-LAYERED
FOCACCIA

Just as focaccia is cresting a wave of popularity and recognition, along comes a whole new school of filled and layered *focacce*. What they have in common is that they all begin with focaccia dough. In some the focaccia dough is rolled out like pastry to enclose a savory filling, while others begin by slicing a fully baked focaccia in half, filling and putting it back in the oven to warm the interior.

SEVERAL FAMOUS FILLED FOCACCE COME FROM LIGURIA: TWO ARE FROM THE FISHING towns of Recco and Varese Ligure outside Genoa, where extremely fine layers of dough enclose a local buttery cheese, while Nicola in the southern reaches of the region makes a pliant focaccia dough that is carpeted with handfuls of basil, rolled up like a jelly roll, baked, and sliced into thin wedges.

IN SOUTHERN ITALY IT IS OFTEN DIFFICULT TO DISTINGUISH FOCACCIA FROM STUFFED PIZZA. Puglia serves two-crusted *focacce* bursting with mussels, with onions, with leeks and black olives. Calabrians fill their *focacce* with broccoli and sausage or cheese and vegetables, while a wealth of choices in Sicily includes a particularly delicious strudel-like focaccia filled with eggplant and tomatoes.

EVEN CALZONE CAN SEEM LIKE A FOCACCIA. ACCORDING TO PROFESSOR LUIGI SADA, THE foremost expert on the food of Puglia, one of several meanings of the term calzone is a disc of dough containing a great variety of ingredients that can range from cheese to onions, anchovies to salame. The only difference between the two is that the calzone is folded in half before being baked. The term calzone first appeared in Bisceglie in 1400 and, while the fillings vary according to local traditions and the seasons, the term has remained constant for centuries.

NOW THAT YOU'VE MASTERED FLAT FOCACCIA, HERE ARE SOME FILLED FOCACCE AND SOME *focacce* for filling.

Filled Focaccia
FOCACCIA RIPIENA

❦

While clever Tuscans have been eating filled focacce for centuries, we are only beginning to realize that focaccia is every bit as versatile as bread and can be served in a multitude of ways. Make focaccia in any size that inspires you, from individual 3-, 4-, or 6-inch discs that can fit in the palm of your hand to 12-inch circles that will feed a small group. When you are ready to eat, cut the focacce in half crosswise, fill them with the ingredients of your dreams, and warm them in the oven to melt the milky cheeses.

Basic Focaccia (page 32) or Focaccia from Genoa (page 34) made into two 12-inch discs

3 to 4 tablespoons Creamy Cheese Spread (page 94) or olive oil

12 to 18 very thin slices prosciutto

8 to 12 ounces best-quality mozzarella, finely sliced

❧ Preheat the oven to 400°F. Cut the focaccia in half crosswise and spread one side with the creamy cheese spread or olive oil. Fill the interiors with the sliced prosciutto and mozzarella. Place on a lightly oiled baking sheet and set in the oven for 12 to 15 minutes, until the cheese is melting inside and bubbling slightly. Cut into wedges and eat immediately.

❧ Makes two 12-inch discs; serves 10 to 12

VARIATION: To make 3- or 4-inch *focaccine:* To shape these smaller discs, divide the dough into 15 or 12 equal pieces and shape each into a ball. Place each ball on one of 2 oiled or parchment paper–lined baking sheets and flatten and stretch each dough ball into a 3- or 4-inch round. The doughs will resist, so cover them with a towel and let them relax for 10 minutes, then stretch the dough some more. Cover again and let rise 45 minutes to 1 hour, or until well puffed. Bake as directed.

❧ Makes fifteen 3-inch or twelve 4-inch focaccine

VARIATIONS: Use speck (smoked prosciutto) or bresaola (salt-cured air-dried beef) in place of the prosciutto. Substitute 3 cups ricotta cheese seasoned with salt and sprinkles of hot red pepper flakes for the prosciutto and cheese.

Sicilian Focaccia
FOCACCIA SICILIANA

❦

Sicilian focaccia is often treated like street food and eaten out of hand as a snack. One of Palermo's most famous stopping places, the Antica Focacceria di San Francesco, actually evolved into a restaurant from much humbler beginnings, but it still serves a focaccia filled with milza, or beef spleen, that has been much sought after for centuries. Garibaldi ate his mixed with fresh ricotta and grated caciocavallo cheese. At the other end of the spectrum are much more refined and elegant focacce such as this one from Modica, which is a sort of strudel that encloses a tasty mixture of eggplant, onions, and tomatoes.

DOUGH
Basic Focaccia dough (page 32), set out for the first rise
FILLING
4 small or 2 medium Italian eggplants
Sea salt
6 tablespoons olive oil
2 garlic cloves
2 onions, sliced
2 ripe tomatoes, peeled, seeded, and chopped
4 ounces (1 cup) grated provolone or Parmesan cheese
Freshly ground black pepper
1 to 2 tablespoons olive oil
INTERIOR AND TOPPING
1½ tablespoons olive oil

❧ While the dough is rising, peel and slice the eggplants. Place them in a colander, sprinkle with salt, and leave to drain for 1 hour. Pat the slices dry and cut into small dice. Warm 3 tablespoons of the olive oil in a large sauté pan or heavy skillet with the garlic; add the eggplant and sauté until golden, being careful not to let the garlic burn. Remove the garlic cloves. Meanwhile, heat the remaining 3 tablespoons of olive oil in a medium sauté pan or heavy skillet and sauté the sliced onions over medium-low heat until translucent, about 15 minutes. Add the tomatoes and cook for 10 minutes. Stir in the eggplant, mix well, and set aside to cool. Stir in the grated cheese and add salt and pepper to taste.

❧ Preheat the oven to 425°F with a baking stone inside, if you have one.

❧ Shaping and second rise. On a lightly floured work surface, roll the dough into a 12 x 16-inch rectangle.

Divide it in half vertically and lightly oil each piece of dough. Divide the filling in half and spread each portion like a thick paste over the top of the dough, leaving a 1-inch margin all around. Trim the edges so they are even. First turn up the short sides and then fold the long sides over the filling, sealing well where they overlap in the center. Pat each rectangle flat to distribute the filling evenly. Line a 10½ x 15½-inch rimless baking sheet with parchment paper. Carefully move each focaccia and set it, seam side down, on the lined baking sheet. Once again pat the top flat and neaten the sides so that they are even. Cover with a towel and let rest for 20 minutes.

❧ Baking. Brush the tops of the dough with oil, place the pans directly on the stone, and bake the *focacce* for about 20 minutes; reduce the temperature to 375°F and bake another 5 to 8 minutes, or until the *focacce* are golden. Very carefully slide the *focacce* off the baking sheets onto a rack. Serve warm or at room temperature.

❧ *Makes two 4½ x 14-inch filled* focacce; *serves 8 to 10*

Basil-filled Spiral Focaccia
SFOGLIERATA

Vittoria Lorenzini, who taught me to make this picturesque basil-filled spiral, assures me that it is a true focaccia although it certainly doesn't look like one. I'd describe it as a delicious dough wrapped around the dense layer of basil leaves that carpets its interior. The sfoglierata is fantastic eaten warm—the fragrance of basil perfumes the air—although it keeps a full 2 days wrapped in a plastic bag. I can't think of a more surprising or sensational addition to a buffet table.

DOUGH

2½ teaspoons (1 package) active dry yeast

½ cup warm water, 105° to 115°F

½ cup plus 2 tablespoons water, room temperature

½ cup mild-tasting extra-virgin olive oil, preferably from Liguria

3¾ cups (500 grams) unbleached all-purpose flour

1½ teaspoons sea salt

FILLING

2 to 3 tablespoons light extra-virgin olive oil, preferably from Liguria

1 large bunch fresh basil, about 1½ to 2 cups tightly packed leaves

TOPPING

1 tablespoon light extra-virgin olive oil, preferably from Liguria

❧ Whisk the yeast into the warm water in a large mixing or mixer bowl; let stand until creamy, about 10 minutes. Stir in the room-temperature water and the oil. If you are making the dough by hand, combine the flour and the salt, add them in 2 additions, and mix until the dough comes together well. Knead on a lightly floured work surface for 4 to 5 minutes, let the dough rest briefly, and finish kneading for another minute or two. The dough will be soft and as delicate as an ear lobe.

❧ If you are using a heavy-duty electric mixer, use the paddle attachment to mix the flour and salt into the yeast mixture until they form a dough. Change to the dough hook and knead for 2 to 3 minutes, or until the dough is as tender as an ear lobe.

❧ First rise. Place the dough in a lightly oiled container, cover it tightly with plastic wrap, and let rise until doubled, about 1 hour to 1 hour and 15 minutes.

❧ Shaping and second rise. Turn the dough out on a lightly floured work surface and roll it with a lightly floured rolling pin into a 12 x 18-inch rectangle that is about ¼ inch thick. The dough will roll out easily and repair easily, if it should it tear. To fill, paint the 2 to 3 tablespoons of olive oil over the top of the dough—be sure to brush it thoroughly, even liberally—and then cover the surface with a thick carpet of basil leaves. Roll up the dough from the long end, like a jelly roll. Oil a 10 x 4-inch angel-food tube pan very well and slip the dough into it, seam-side down. Don't be concerned if the 2 ends of the roll don't touch; they will after the second rise. Cover the dough with a towel and let rise until doubled, about 1 to 1½ hours.

❧ Baking. At least 30 minutes before you plan to bake, preheat the oven to 400°F with a baking stone inside, if you have one. Brush the top of the *sfoglierata* with 1 tablespoon of olive oil. Place the pan directly on the stone and bake until golden, about 40 minutes. Let

cool for 15 or 20 minutes, then slide the blade of a long thin knife or spatula between the *sfoglierata* and the pan sides and the center tube to loosen it. (If the pan has a removable bottom, remove it from the sides, then slide the knife between the pan bottom and *sfoglierata* to release it.) Place on a rack. Serve warm.

❧ *Makes one 10-inch focaccia; serves 8 to 10*

Little Focacce for Filling
FOCACCINE

W hat's chic to eat in Forte dei Marmi, that very chic Tuscan resort town on the Mediterranean? Hordes of hungry people queue up at all hours of day and night for this thin focaccia that is sliced open horizontally, spread with any number of tantalizing fillings, closed, heated briefly, and served up.

DOUGH
Basic Focaccia dough (page 32) or Schiacciata with Starter dough (page 36), made through the first rise
TOPPING
Olive oil

❧ Shaping. Divide the dough into 4 equal pieces and spread each one in an oiled 9-inch pie pan. Use wet or oiled hands to press each one out to fill the bottom of the pan. If the dough resists, cover with a towel, let it relax for 10 minutes, then press and stretch again until it reaches the edges. Cover with a towel and leave until the dough is full of air bubbles, 45 minutes to 1 hour. Just before baking, dimple the dough gently with your fingertips and sprinkle the top with olive oil.

❧ Baking. At least 30 minutes before you are ready to bake, preheat the oven to 425°F with a baking stone inside, if you have one. Set 2 pans aside and cover, place the other 2 pans directly on the preheated stone and spray the oven walls and floor with cold water from a spritzer bottle 3 times in the first 10 minutes. Bake until the tops of the dough are golden and the crust shrinks slightly away from the sides of the pan, about 20 minutes. Immediately slide the *focaccine* out of the pans and cool on a rack to room temperature. Repeat with the other doughs. Slice the *focaccine* in half crosswise, spread the filling of your choice inside, place it in a hot oven, heat for 5 to 8 minutes, and slice into wedges to serve.

❧ *Makes four 9-inch round* focaccine; *serves 8 to 10*
VARIATION: To make 5-inch *focaccine*: Divide the dough into 8 equal pieces and shape each into a ball. Place the balls of dough on oiled or parchment paper–lined rimless baking sheets and cover with towels. Let stand for 10 minutes, then press and stretch each into a 5-inch disc. Bake as directed. Makes eight 5-inch *focaccine*.

Cheese Focaccia from Varese Ligure
FOCACCIA AL FORMAGGIO

R ecco and Varese Ligure are towns outside Genoa famous for making focaccia in which fine veils of dough enclose a creamy local cheese. This sublime version comes from Varese Ligure, where the dough is made with a tiny amount of yeast. Don't be sparing with the cheese.

DOUGH

½ cup plus 1 tablespoon warm water, 105° to 115°F

½ teaspoon active dry yeast

2½ tablespoons extra-virgin olive oil, preferably from
    Liguria

1¾ cups plus 2 tablespoons (250 grams) unbleached all-
    purpose flour

¾ teaspoon sea salt

FILLING AND TOPPING

About 3½ tablespoons mild-tasting extra-virgin olive oil,
    preferably from Liguria

6 ounces creamy Italian cheese, such as Stracchino or
    Taleggio, thinly sliced

Generous pinch of sea salt

❧ Place the warm water in a medium mixing bowl or mixer bowl, sprinkle the yeast over it, and whisk it in; let stand until creamy, about 10 minutes. Stir in the olive oil. If you are making the dough by hand, combine the flour and salt and use a wooden spoon to stir them into the yeast mixture in 2 additions. Mix until a dough is formed, then knead on a lightly floured work surface until the dough is firm and elastic, about 5 to 6 minutes.

❧ If you are using a heavy-duty electric mixer, set the paddle attachment in place, mix the flour and salt into the yeast mixture, and stir for about 2 minutes, or until a smooth dough is formed. Change to the dough hook and knead for 2 minutes at low speed to produce a firm dough.

❧ First rise. Place the dough in a lightly oiled container, cover tightly with plastic wrap, and let rise for a maximum of 30 minutes.

❧ Shaping and second rise. Cut a 10-inch circle out of parchment paper and place it in the bottom of a 9-inch baking pan; the edges will come up the sides slightly. Divide the dough in half. Set each piece on a lightly floured work surface and roll each piece into a 9-inch circle with a lightly floured rolling pin roll. Lay 1 circle inside the baking pan and brush it well with 1 tablespoon of olive oil. Arrange the cheese over it, leaving a 1-inch border, and brush the edge with water. Lay the second circle of dough on top of the cheese. Trim the edges with scissors or a paring knife and seal them well, pressing them together firmly to prevent the cheese from escaping during the baking. Cover with a towel and let rise for 30 minutes.

❧ Baking. At least 30 minutes before you are ready to bake, preheat the oven to 450°F with a stone, if you have one. Dimple the top of the dough with your fingertips, paint it with 2 tablespoons of the olive oil, and sprinkle with a generous pinch of sea salt. Prick the top crust with the tines of a fork and, if the dough begins to develop bubbles, prick them with a skewer. Place the pan directly on the stone and bake for 10 minutes, then reduce the heat to 350°F and continue baking for 10 to 12 more minutes, or until the top is golden. Immediately brush the remaining ½ tablespoon of olive oil over the top, cut into wedges, and serve at once. You also may serve the focaccia warm, or reheat and serve later.

❧ *Makes one 9-inch round filled focaccia; serves 4 to 6*

Focaccia with Mussels

FOCACCIA ALLE COZZE

This focaccia is filled with masses of mussels. It can hold center stage as the main dish at a lunch or supper, but is as easily served as part of an antipasto. The filling has a double life: Turn any leftovers into a pasta sauce or stir them into risotto.

DOUGH

½ recipe Basic Focaccia dough (page 32), set out to rise for 1¼ hours

FILLING

2 pounds fresh mussels

4 tablespoons olive oil

3 garlic cloves: 1 whole, 2 minced

¼ cup dry white wine

2 fresh tomatoes, peeled, seeded, and chopped

3 tablespoons finely chopped fresh flat-leaf parsley

¼ teaspoon sea salt

Freshly ground black pepper

TOPPING

About 1 tablespoon extra-virgin olive oil

❧ Preheat the oven to 400°F. While the focaccia is rising, scrub the mussels under cold running water. Scrub off any barnacles and slice away the beards with a paring knife. Wash the mussels in several changes of water and throw away any that remain open.

❧ Warm 2 tablespoons of the olive oil and the whole garlic clove in a wide shallow pan for 3 to 4 minutes; add the white wine and mussels, cover, and cook over high heat, shaking frequently, until the shells open,

about 4 to 5 minutes. Immediately remove from the heat. Hold the shells over the pan as you remove the meat so the juices fall back into the pan. Place the mussels in a bowl and discard the shells. Strain the cooking liquid left in the pan through a sieve lined with cheesecloth or paper towels into a bowl. Set the liquid aside.

❧ Pour the remaining 2 tablespoons olive oil into the pot in which you cooked the mussels, add the 2 minced garlic cloves, and cook briefly over low-medium heat, 2 to 3 minutes. Add the tomatoes, parsley, salt, and pepper and cook over low heat for about 10 minutes. Return the mussels to the pan along with their reserved cooking juices and continue cooking just long enough to let the flavors mingle, about 2 minutes. Remove from the heat and cool. Drain the liquids thoroughly (save them for another dish) so the bottom of the focaccia won't be gummy.

❧ Divide the focaccia dough in half. Press out 1 half with your fingers to cover the bottom and slightly overlap the sides of a well-oiled 9-inch pie pan. You may also use a rolling pin to roll the dough out on a lightly floured work surface to form an 11-inch circle. Brush a light wash of oil over the dough and fill with the mussel mixture. Roll the remaining piece of dough into a 9-inch circle. Lay it on top of the filling. Trim the edges of any excess dough and, with your fingers, crimp the 2 layers of dough together well to seal in the filling and close the focaccia. Brush the top of the dough with the olive oil and pierce it with the tines of a fork every inch or so to allow steam to escape.

❧ Baking. Place the pan in the oven and bake until the top is golden, about 22 to 25 minutes. Leave in the pan until the bottom crust is firm and cool enough to ease it out without difficulty. Slice into wedges to serve.

❧ *Makes one 9-inch round filled focaccia; serves 6*

FILLINGS FOR FOCACCE AND FOCACCINE

OCACCIA AND FOCACCINE ARE WONDERFUL
eaten plain, but they can also be filled for a fantastic snack. All you have to do is slice a focaccia or *focaccina* in half, spread it with a creamy filling, put it back into the oven for a good blast of heat, and serve it right away.

ALWAYS PAINT A WASH OF OLIVE OIL ON THE INSIDES OF THE CUT FOCACCIA BEFORE YOU fill it. With *focaccine*, begin with the Creamy Cheese Spread (page 94). Use any of the fillings on the pages that follow, or exercise your ingenuity as the Italians do and dream up glorious combinations to satisfy your hunger and your whole being.

THESE FEW IDEAS ARE HERE ONLY TO SPUR YOUR GASTRONOMIC IMAGINATION: SLIDE SOME prosciutto, sliced tomatoes, and shreds of tangy mozzarella cheese inside a focaccia or *focaccine,* warm in the oven, and serve when the mozzarella is soft and melting. Fill the interior with tomatoes, mozzarella cheese, and a handful of finely shredded basil leaves. Spread the interior of *focaccine* with a puree of artichoke and top with slices of the best available ham. Brush the insides of a sliced focaccia with Creamy Cheese Spread, sprinkle with ground cloves and black pepper, and warm it in the oven. Spread split *focaccine* with creamy cheese filling then dapple it with a layer of the thinnest prosciutto and a thick covering of sautéed mushrooms.

PEEK INTO YOUR PANTRY OR REFRIGERATOR, PAY A VISIT TO YOUR GROCERY OR DELICATESSEN. You could top a layer of sautéed chard with dabs of creamy stracchino, taleggio, or nutmeg-scented ricotta cheese. Or slather creamy cheese spread over *focaccine,* scatter some caramelized white onions or roasted red peppers on top, and set it all in the oven for a brief blast of heat. Cast your eyes over the entire panoply of Italian ingredients and let *fantasia* inspire you to invent your own fillings and flavor combinations for focaccia and *focaccine*.

THE FILLINGS IN THE FOLLOWING PAGES CAN BE SPREAD INSIDE THIN FOCACCETTE THAT HAVE been split in half as well as inside other rolls and breads.

Mushroom Filling
CONDIMENTO AI FUNGHI
❦

Thick as a paste, heady as wild mushrooms: Here is a tantalizing filling to spread inside thin focaccine.

½ ounce dried porcini mushrooms
3 tablespoons extra-virgin olive oil
3 white onions, finely chopped
1 pound brown or cremini mushrooms, finely chopped
½ cup peeled, seeded, and finely chopped Italian plum
    tomatoes
3 tablespoons finely chopped fresh flat-leaf parsley
Sea salt
Freshly ground black pepper

❧ Soak the dried porcini mushrooms in warm water to cover for 1 hour. Lift them out, rinse them if they are still slightly gritty, and squeeze them, letting any extra liquid fall into the soaking water. Dry them. Strain the soaking liquid through a sieve lined with cheesecloth or with a double layer of paper towels and placed over a bowl. Chop the porcini mushrooms finely; reserve the liquid.

❧ Heat the oil in a large sauté pan or heavy skillet over medium heat, reduce the heat to low, and cook the onions until translucent and soft, about 15 to 20 minutes. Stir in the porcini and cook for 5 minutes. Stir in the fresh mushrooms with ¼ to ½ cup of the reserved mushroom liquid, or enough to moisten them; simmer uncovered for 30 minutes. Add the tomatoes and simmer another 10 to 15 minutes, or until the liquid has cooked away and the mixture is thick and concen-trated. Stir in the parsley, and salt and pepper to taste and cook 3 minutes longer. Let cool.

❧ Makes 2 cups, enough to fill 4 focaccine

Onion Filling
CONDIMENTO DI CIPOLLE
❦

This wonderful filling for focaccine has a slightly sweet taste that plays against the delicate bite of balsamic vinegar. I am supremely grateful to Maurizio and Massimo and their mother, Rosa Binelli, at the Pizzeria Marconi in Forte dei Marmi for sharing the secret of how they make it.

2 white onions, sliced ¼ inch thick
3 tablespoons extra-virgin olive oil
½ teaspoon balsamic vinegar

❧ Preheat the oven to 350°F. Bring a medium pot of water to the boil, add the onion slices, and boil uncovered for 2 minutes. Remove the onions with a slotted spoon, drain well, spread them out on a tea towel, and pat dry.

❧ Transfer the onions to a lightly oiled baking sheet and bake for 25 to 30 minutes, letting them dry slowly and being sure that they are pale and golden when finished. Remove the onion slices from the oven and place them in a bowl. Toss the warm onions with the oil and vinegar. This condiment will keep at least 1 week in the refrigerator.

❧ Makes 2 cups, enough to fill 4 focaccine

Creamy Cheese Spread
CREMA DI FORMAGGIO
❧

When I first tasted the creamy cheese mixture that focaccia makers in Forte dei Marmi spread on the inside of focaccine, I wanted to eat it alone on a spoon. Smooth, voluptuous and slightly tangy, it is amazingly versatile, a perfect substitute for mayonnaise in any number of dishes. Look for the little golden circular packages of Bel Paese and be sure to use the creamy variety of Gorgonzola cheese called Dolcelatte, not the longer-aged, more piquant one. This spread keeps well in the refrigerator for more than a week, although it's hard to imagine that it won't have disappeared by then.

> 4 ounces Bel Paese processed cheese spread or Bel Paese cheese, diced, room temperature
> 2 tablespoons butter, room temperature
> 2 tablespoons heavy (whipping) cream, room temperature
> ¾ teaspoon Gorgonzola cheese, Dolcelatte variety

❧ Mix all the ingredients in a blender or food processor, or mash the Bel Paese cheese spread or cheese in a mixing bowl with a wooden spoon and beat in the butter, cream, and Gorgonzola cheese.

❧ *Makes ½ cup, enough for 4 focaccine*

Artichoke Filling
CONDIMENTO DI CARCIOFI
❧

This creamy artichoke filling for focaccine is deliciously rich in flavor although not in calories or complexity.

> 5 tablespoons olive oil
> 1 onion, finely sliced
> One 10-ounce package frozen artichoke hearts, thawed, drained, and sliced
> 1 teaspoon sea salt, or to taste
> A few drops of balsamic vinegar

❧ Warm 2 tablespoons of the olive oil in a heavy skillet over very low heat and cook the onions for 30 minutes, or until soft, translucent, and almost melting. Stir in the sliced artichoke hearts and cook over low heat for another 3 to 5 minutes. Add the salt and let cool slightly.

❧ Purée the mixture in a blender or food processor. Add just enough balsamic vinegar to bring out the taste of the artichokes and process briefly to mix well.

❧ *Makes enough to fill 4 to 6 focaccine*

Clam Filling
CONDIMENTO DI VONGOLE
❀

Oh for the clams of Italy that taste deliciously of the sea! The arselle that give their lovely flavor to this filling are as tiny as a baby's fingernail. Use the freshest clams you can find and cut them into fine dice.

2 pounds fresh clams, preferably littlenecks
⅓ cup water
⅓ cup dry white wine
¼ cup olive oil
1 white onion, finely minced
1 tablespoon minced garlic
3 tablespoons chopped fresh flat-leaf parsley
1 tomato, peeled, seeded, and finely chopped
Pinch of hot pepper flakes

❧ Soak the clams in a basin of cold water for 10 minutes. Scrub each one with a stiff brush, then drain and refill the basin with more cold water and scrub the clams again, making sure you have eliminated all the dirt and sand. Drain. Discard any clams that don't close.

❧ Pour the water and wine into a large deep pot, add the clams, cover tightly, and turn the heat to the highest setting. Shake the pot to move the clams around and cook for 5 to 8 minutes until they open. Transfer the clams to a large bowl as they open their shells. Strain the cooking liquid through a sieve lined with cheesecloth or a double thickness of paper towels into a medium bowl. Hold the shells over the bowl while you detach the clam meat and let any juice remaining in the shells fall into the bowl. Strain the juices again if you think they are at all sandy. Put the clam meat on a cutting board and chop it very fine.

❧ Warm the olive oil in a medium sauté pan or heavy skillet, add the onion and cook until it is pale and translucent, about 15 minutes. Add the garlic and parsley, and cook for another 3 to 4 minutes, taking care that the garlic stays golden and does not brown. Stir in the chopped tomato and cook for 5 or 6 minutes. Add the strained clam liquid and hot pepper flakes and cook over medium heat until the liquid has almost evaporated. Add the chopped clams and sauté briefly.

❧ Makes enough to fill 4 focaccine

Sweet Pepper Filling

CONDIMENTO AI PEPERONI

✿

Sweet peppers come in brilliant colors that dazzle the eye and in flavors so sweet that they bewitch the palate. Crimson, buttery yellow, gold, and deep purple, they are intense enough to have leapt off a canvas by van Gogh and into the kitchen and a waiting focaccina.

> 3 sweet red and/or yellow peppers
> 3 tablespoons extra-virgin olive oil
> 1 red onion, diced
> 1 to 1½ teaspoons sea salt

❧ Roast the peppers by broiling them on a broiler pan about 3 inches from the heat or by roasting them over a high gas flame until they are well seared. The skins should be uniformly charred and blistered so they are easy to pull away from the flesh. Place the peppers in a paper or plastic bag, close it tightly, and set aside for 15 to 30 minutes. Then cut the peppers in half, remove their stems, ribs, and seeds, and peel off the skin. Slice the peppers ½ inch thick, then cut into matchstick lengths, 3 to 4 inches.

❧ Meanwhile, warm the olive oil over low heat in a large sauté pan or heavy skillet, add the diced onion, and cook very slowly over very low heat for 25 to 30 minutes, or until it is limp and translucent. Stir in the pepper strips and continue to cook over very low heat for another 15 to 20 minutes. Transfer to a bowl to cool. Add the salt and mix well.

❧ *Makes enough to fill 4 focaccine*

SWEET FOCACCIA

OR CENTURIES BAKERS HAVE PLUNGED SUGAR, eggs, milk, nuts, and dried fruits into the modest and humble doughs of everyday to create the tastes of celebration. No one knows when it first occured to them that they could turn their legendary sweet tooth loose on focaccia as well as great festival breads, so there is no record of the moment they transformed a humble savory into a sublime sugary treat. Inspired, those bakers crammed fat raisins and fatter figs, toasty walnuts and hazelnuts, even Sangiovese grapes into focaccia destined for breakfast tables, mid-afternoon *merende,* and dessert any time.

A SWEET FOCACCIA CAN BE AS SIMPLE AS A DOUGH WITH SUGAR ADDED OR AS COMPLICATED as two liqueur-spiked brioche-like layers enclosing handfuls of ripe grapes or flavor-filled raisins. It can have the rustic crunch of cornmeal or the aristocratic smoothness of butter, the slightest tang of saffron or the brightness of orange zest. It can be as fine as the thinnest pizza dough covered with fresh summer fruits, or it can be a bit thick and topped with creamy, anise-scented elderflowers.

SWEET FOCACCIA HAS BECOME A DISTINCTIVE CATEGORY ALL ITS OWN, A LOVELY SUGAR-flavored treat that embraces the informality of the countryside and the elegance of city life. It's a hit at any hour served with caffé or with wine. I wouldn't be surprised to see it become a new craze in America, where it might even give fast food and the sweet tooth a good name.

Sweet Focaccia Dough

FOCACCIA DOLCE

W hat's the difference between regular focaccia and focaccia dough that is sweet? About ¼ cup of sugar and the element of surprise. As strange as it may seem, sweet focaccia is absolutely delicious. The crust is super thin, the fruit should be ripe and juicy, and focaccia becomes an amazingly light dessert for any meal.

SPONGE

½ cup warm water, 105° to 115°F

1 tablespoon sugar

1 teaspoon active dry yeast

¾ cup (100 grams) unbleached all-purpose flour

DOUGH

1 teaspoon active dry yeast

1 cup warm water, 105° to 115°F

2 tablespoons olive oil

Sponge, above

3 tablespoons sugar

3¼ cups (450 grams) unbleached all-purpose flour

1½ teaspoons sea salt

FOR BRUSHING THE DOUGH

Olive oil

❧ To make the sponge: Place the warm water and sugar in a small bowl, sprinkle the yeast over them, and whisk it in; let stand until foamy, about 5 to 10 minutes. Stir in the flour to form a soft dough. Cover tightly with plastic wrap and let stand until very bubbly and doubled, about 30 to 45 minutes.

❧ To make the dough: Whisk the yeast into the warm water in a large mixing or mixer bowl and let stand until creamy, about 5 to 10 minutes. Stir in the olive oil and beat in the sponge. If you are making the dough by hand, add the sugar and 1 cup of the flour to the yeast mixture, using a whisk to keep lumps from forming. With a wooden spoon, stir in the salt and the remaining flour in 2 additions and stir until the dough comes together. Knead on a lightly floured surface until soft and velvety, about 10 minutes.

❧ If you are making the dough in a heavy-duty mixer, use the paddle attachment to add the sugar, flour, and salt to the yeast mixture; mix for 1 to 2 minutes, or until a dough is formed. Change to the dough hook and knead at medium speed until the dough is soft, velvety, and slightly sticky, 3 to 4 minutes.

❧ First rise. Place the dough in a lightly oiled container, cover it tightly with plastic wrap, and let rise until doubled, about 1¼ hours.

❧ Thirty to 45 minutes before you plan to bake, preheat the oven to 450°F with a baking stone inside, if you have one.

❧ Shaping and second rise. When the dough has finished its initial rise, divide it into 3 equal pieces. Using a rolling pin, roll out each one on a lightly floured work surface to a ⅛-inch thickness. Set each on a lightly oiled 12-inch perforated pizza pan and build up a slightly thicker edge. You may also shape them into rounds and place them on lightly floured or cornmeal-sprinkled parchment paper–lined peels or baking sheets. Cover with towels and let rise for 20 minutes.

❧ Assembling and baking. Work with one dough at a time, keeping the other two covered. Brush 1 teaspoon of olive oil over the surface of one dough. Arrange whatever fruits and nuts the recipe calls for and press them firmly in place with the back of a spoon. Drizzle with whatever liqueur or liquid the recipe calls for. Brush the raised edges with a little olive oil. Place the pan directly on the stone and bake for 12 to 15 minutes, or until the edges and bottom of the focaccia are golden brown. If you are shaping the dough on parchment paper, you can place the dough and paper directly on the stone, then pull out the paper when the dough has set, about 8 minutes. Remove the focaccia with a peel and let cool very briefly. Remove from pans if using. Serve hot or cool briefly on racks and serve at a warm room temperature. Repeat to bake the remaining *focacce*.

❧ *Makes three 12-inch round* focacce; *serves 10 to 12*
VARIATION: Shape the dough into six 6-inch discs.

Sweet Focaccia with Oranges, Raisins, and Nuts
FOCACCIA DOLCE ALLA FRUTTA
❀

H*ere's my way of making sure I can have a super-thin focaccia with fruit all year long.*

DOUGH
Sweet Focaccia Dough *(page 100), made through the first rise*
TOPPING
½ *cup raisins*
3 *tablespoons* Curaçao
½ *cup walnuts*
3 *to* 4 *tablespoons olive oil*
2 *oranges, finely sliced*

❧ While the dough is rising, soak the raisins in the Curaçao for 30 minutes, then drain, reserving the liqueur. Toast the walnuts in a preheated 350°F oven for 10 to 12 minutes and set aside to cool.

❧ Shaping and second rise. About 30 to 45 minutes before you plan to bake, preheat the oven to 450°F with a baking stone inside, if you have one. When the dough has concluded its initial rise, divide the dough into 3 equal pieces and, with a rolling pin, roll each out on a lightly floured work surface to a ⅛-inch thickness. Place each piece on a lightly oiled 12-inch perforated pizza pan and build up a slightly thicker edge. You may also shape the rounds free-form and place them on lightly floured parchment paper–lined peels or oiled rimless baking sheets. Cover them with a towel and let rise for 20 minutes.

❧ Assembling and baking. Work with one focaccia at a time, keeping the others covered with a towel. Brush 1 teaspoon of olive oil over the surface of the focaccia. Arrange the orange slices in concentric circles on the dough, sprinkle the raisins and walnuts in the spaces in between and press them firmly in place, using the back of a spoon. Drizzle the reserved Curaçao over the top. Brush the raised edges of the focaccia with a little olive oil. Place the pan directly on the stone and bake until the edges and bottom of the focaccia are golden brown, 12 to 15 minutes. If you are using parchment paper, you can set the dough and paper directly on the stone, then slip the paper out after about 8 minutes, once the dough has set. Use a peel to take the focaccia from the the oven. Immediately brush the edges of the focaccia with a bit of olive oil, and transfer to a rack from the pan, if you are using one. Serve hot or very

warm. Repeat to top and bake the remaining *focacce*.

❧ *Makes three 12-inch round* focacce; *serves 10 to 12*

VARIATION: Shape into six 6-inch discs.

Sweet Focaccia with Fruit

FOCACCIA DOLCE ALLA FRUTTA FRESCA

❦

This sweet focaccia may look like pizza, but its topping isn't likely to be found anywhere near Naples. When I first saw sweet focaccia listed on the menu of a Tuscan restaurant that specializes in focaccia, the waiter looked as if he wished I hadn't brought up the subject and he certainly didn't encourage me to order it. "Un po' particolare" ("a special taste"), was how he put it, but I'm glad I didn't let him talk me out of it. Now I'm a major believer in very thin focacce topped with fruit.

Please overcome whatever scepticism you have and try the amazing combination of fruit and focaccia. You may use the fruits of your choice, although nothing is better than concentric circles of peaches, nectarines, and/or plums. If you can't find anise-flavored Sambuca liqueur, use anisette. This focaccia is especially delicious when made with a very thin crust.

DOUGH

Sweet Focaccia Dough (page 100), made through the first rise

TOPPING

2 to 3 tablespoons olive oil, preferably from Liguria

2 large or 3 medium peeled peaches or nectarines or 4 to 5 plums, pitted and sliced finely

1½ tablespoons Sambuca liqueur

❧ At least 30 to 45 minutes before you plan to bake, preheat the oven to 425°F with a baking stone inside, if you have one. When the dough has finished its first rise, divide and shape it and set it out for the second rise as directed.

❧ Assembling and baking. Work with one dough at a time, keeping the others covered with a towel. Brush 1 teaspoon of the olive oil over the surface of the focaccia and cover it with the fruit slices arranged in concentric circles. Drizzle the Sambuca liqueur over the top. Brush the raised edges of the focaccia with a little more olive oil. Place the pan directly on the stone and bake until the edges and bottom of the focaccia are golden brown, 12 to 15 minutes. If you are using parchment paper, you can place the dough and parchment directly on the stone and then slip the paper out after about 8 minutes, when the dough has set. Using a peel or a rimless cookie sheet, slide the focaccia out of the oven onto a rack, immediately brush the edges with a bit of olive oil, and serve hot or at a very warm room temperature. If using a pizza pan, slide the focaccia immediately out of the pan onto a rack. Repeat to top and bake the remaining *focacce*.

❧ *Makes three 12-inch round* focacce; *serves 10 to 12*

Cornmeal Focaccia with Figs
FOCACCIA AI FICHI

❀

The crunch of cornmeal meets the sweetness of figs in an inspired combination of simple country ingredients. To enjoy the full sweetness that this focaccia can have, save the water in which you soak the figs and use it for making the dough.

DOUGH

8 ounces dried figs, preferably Calmyrna

1½ cups water, room temperature

2½ teaspoons (1 package) active dry yeast

2 tablespoons olive oil

½ cup plus 2 teaspoons (80 grams) cornmeal

3 cups (420 grams) unbleached all-purpose flour

1½ teaspoons sea salt

TOPPING

2 tablespoons olive oil

1 tablespoon turbinado sugar

❧ Soak the figs in the water for 30 minutes. Drain, reserving 1⅓ cups of the water, and coarsely chop the figs. Warm the reserved water to 105° to 115°F. Sprinkle the yeast over the warmed fig water in a large mixing or mixer bowl, whisk it in, and let stand until creamy, about 10 minutes. Stir in the olive oil. If you are making the focaccia by hand, mix together the cornmeal, flour, and salt and add the mixture in 2 additions to the yeast mixture, stirring with a wooden spoon until a dough is formed. Knead on a lightly floured work surface for 8 to 10 minutes, or until the dough is firm and elastic.

❧ If you are using a heavy-duty electric mixer, use the paddle attachment to mix the cornmeal, flour, and salt into the yeast mixture. Change to the dough hook and knead for about 3 minutes, or until the dough is firm and slightly sticky. Knead briefly by hand on a lightly floured surface to eliminate any stickiness.

❧ First rise. Place the dough in a lightly oiled container, cover it tightly with plastic wrap, and let rise until doubled, about 45 minutes.

❧ Shaping and second rise. On a lightly floured work surface, flatten the dough into a 7 or 8 x 14-inch rectangle. Distribute three quarters of the figs over the top, leaving a 1-inch margin around the edges. Fold in all the sides and roll the dough into a ball. Place in an oiled 10½ x 15½-inch baking pan and flatten with the palm of your hand, being careful to keep the figs from poking through the skin of the dough. Press gently on the surface to stretch the dough to fit the bottom of the pan and, when it resists, cover and let stand for 10 minutes. Stretch the dough again until it reaches the edges of the pan. Cover with a towel and let rise until doubled, about 1 hour.

❧ Baking. At least 30 minutes before you plan to bake, preheat the oven to 400°F with a baking stone inside, if you have one. Dimple the dough lightly with your fingertips, drizzle with the olive oil, dot the remaining figs over the top, and sprinkle with the turbinado sugar. Place the pan directly on the stone and bake until the focaccia is golden, about 20 to 25 minutes. Serve warm or at room temperature.

❧ Makes one 10½ x 15½-inch focaccia; serves 6 to 8

Orange-scented Focaccia from Florence

SCHIACCIATA ALLA FIORENTINA

❧

Florentines once ate this sweet focaccia only during Lent, although it hardly seems the food of deprivation. The pinch of saffron is testimony that it dates back to medieval times, but these days bakers tend to omit the rare, slightly tangy spice. This delicacy is perfect for tea and is sensational when toasted for breakfast. One inventive woman I know uses a biscuit cutter to make little rounds, which she serves as a splendid variation on strawberry shortcake.

SPONGE

1 teaspoon active dry yeast

2 tablespoons sugar

¾ cup warm water, 105° to 115°F

¾ cup (100 grams) unbleached all-purpose flour

DOUGH

Sponge, above

2 eggs, room temperature, lightly beaten

½ cup sugar

Grated zest of 2 oranges

½ teaspoon vanilla extract

2 ¾ cups plus 3 tablespoons (400 grams) unbleached all-purpose flour

Pinch of sea salt

Large pinch of powdered saffron

¾ cup (1½ sticks) plus 1 tablespoon unsalted butter or best-quality lard, room temperature, cut into 6 equal pieces

GLAZE

1 egg beaten with 2 teaspoons water

Powdered sugar

❧ To make the sponge: Whisk the yeast and sugar into the warm water in a small bowl and let stand until foamy, about 5 to 10 minutes. Stir in the flour to make a soupy batter. Cover well with plastic wrap and let rise until doubled, about 45 minutes.

❧ Transfer the sponge to a large mixing or mixer bowl. If you are making the dough by hand, use a wooden spoon to stir the eggs, sugar, orange zest, and vanilla into the sponge. Mix together the flour, salt, and saffron and add to the sponge mixture in 2 additions. Stir in the butter or lard 1 piece at a time and beat it in well. Knead by hand on a lightly floured surface until sticky and buttery-feeling but elastic, 13 to 15 minutes.

❧ If you are using a heavy-duty electric mixer, add the eggs, sugar, and orange zest to the sponge and mix thoroughly with the paddle attachment until smooth. Add the flour, salt, and saffron, and mix until the dough comes together. Mix in the butter or lard, 1 piece at a time. Change to the dough hook and knead for 2 minutes on low, then 2 minutes on medium speed, or until the dough is sticky and buttery-feeling but elastic. Knead briefly on a lightly floured work surface until the dough becomes supple and responsive.

❧ First rise. Place the dough in a buttered or oiled container, cover it tightly with plastic wrap, and let rise until doubled, about 2 hours and 15 minutes. The dough will still be soft but it will puff up nicely.

❧ Shaping and second rise. Spread the dough to cover

the bottom of an oiled or buttered 10½ x 15½-inch baking pan. Cover with a towel and let rise until well puffed and just barely doubled, about 1½ hours.

❧ Baking. Thirty minutes before you plan to bake, preheat the oven to 400°F with a baking stone inside, if you have one. Brush the top of the *schiacciata* with the egg-water mixture. Place directly on the stone and bake for 10 minutes, then reduce the temperature to 350°F and continue baking until the top of the *schiacciata* is golden, 12 to 15 minutes more. Remove from the oven, wait 5 minutes, then remove the *schiacciata* from the pan. Cool on a rack for 5 to 10 minutes before sifting powdered sugar over the top. Cut into small squares and serve at room temperature.

❧ *Makes one 10½ x 15½-inch* schiacciata; *serves 10 to 12*

Elderflower Schiacciata
STIACCIATA AL SAMBUCO

*N*either strongly sweet or savory, this schiacciata *tastes subtly of the anise flavor of elderflowers. The elder, or elderberry, shrub belongs to the honeysuckle family, and its white creamy blossoms, picked early to midsummer, are used to make fritters, jam, and even wine and champagne. Should you find elderberry shrubs, be sure to use the blossoms, not the leaves. Natives of the city and countryside of Arezzo count this a traditional favorite and people in the Chianti region of Tuscany often serve it midafternoon with a glass of wine. Elderflower concentrate is available by mail (see Source List), or you may substitute a little Sambuca liqueur.*

DOUGH

⅓ *cup warm water, 105° to 115°F*

2½ *teaspoons (1 package) active dry yeast*

⅔ *cup plus 2 tablespoons water, room temperature*

1 *egg, lightly beaten*

1 *tablespoon olive oil*

2 *tablespoons Elderflower Concentrate or Sambuca liqueur, or ½ cup elderflowers, coarse stems removed*

3¾ *cups (500 grams) unbleached all-purpose flour*

1½ *teaspoons sea salt*

TOPPING

2 *tablespoons olive oil*

2 *tablespoons Elderflower Concentrate or Sambuca liqueur*

½ *to ¾ teaspoon fennel seeds*

❧ Place the warm water in a medium mixing or mixer bowl, sprinkle the yeast over it, and whisk it in; let stand until creamy, about 10 minutes. Stir in the room-temperature water, egg, olive oil, and the elderflower concentrate or Sambuca liqueur. If you are making the dough by hand, mix the flour and salt together and whisk 1 cup into the yeast mixture. With a wooden spoon, mix in the remaining flour in 2 additions until the dough comes together. Knead on a lightly floured surface 8 to 10 minutes, or until firm, elastic, and velvety.

❧ If you are using a heavy-duty electric mixer, add the flour and salt to the yeast mixture and stir with the paddle for 1 to 2 minutes. Change to the dough hook and knead for 2 minutes at low speed and 2 minutes at medium, or until the dough is firm, velvety, and elastic.

❧ First rise. Place the dough in a lightly oiled container, cover it tightly with plastic wrap, and let rise until doubled, 45 minutes to 1 hour.

Shaping and second rise. Divide the dough in half and place each piece in an oiled 9-inch pie pan. Press each piece out to fill the bottom of the pan, but if it resists, cover with a towel, let it relax for 10 minutes, then press and stretch the dough again until it reaches the edges. Cover with towels and let rise until very puffy, about 45 minutes.

Baking. Thirty minutes before you plan to bake, preheat the oven to 400°F with a baking stone inside, if you have one. Just before baking, dimple the top of the doughs with vigor and sprinkle them evenly with the olive oil, concentrate or liqueur, and fennel seeds. Place the pans directly on the stone and bake for 20 to 22 minutes, or until the dough is a deep golden color. Immediately remove from the pans, transfer to a rack, and let cool. Serve at room temperature.

Makes two 9-inch round schiacciate; serves 8 to 10

Schiacciata Bursting with Grapes
SCHIACCIATA ALL'UVA

At the time of the grape harvest in Tuscany, not every Sangiovese grape is carried off and crushed to make Chianti Classico wine. Clever bakers scoop up armloads that they press between layers of gloriously sweetened bread dough and then bury under a blizzard of crunchy sugar. When I tasted this particular version with its aniseeds and Sambuca liqueur, I couldn't wait to learn the secrets of the baker. If you can't find Sambuca, an anise-flavored liqueur, you can substitute anisette, although it isn't quite as smooth or as sweet.

SPONGE

2 teaspoons active dry yeast

¼ cup sugar

1 cup warm water, 105° to 115°F

1 cup plus 2 teaspoons (150 grams) unbleached all-purpose flour

DOUGH

3 tablespoons Sambuca liqueur

3 tablespoons warm water, 105° to 115°F

2½ cups (350 grams) unbleached all-purpose flour

1 teaspoon sea salt

2 teaspoons aniseeds, slightly crushed

½ cup (1 stick) unsalted butter or best-quality lard, room temperature, cut into 8 equal pieces

TOPPING

3 pounds seedless Red Flame grapes stemmed and washed

About 6 tablespoons turbinado sugar

Sambuca liqueur

To make the sponge: Whisk the yeast and sugar into the warm water in a large mixing or mixer bowl and let stand until frothy, about 10 minutes. Stir in the flour in 2 additions, then cover tightly with plastic wrap and let stand until bubbling and doubled, about 30 to 45 minutes.

To make the dough: Beat the liqueur and water into the sponge. If you are making the dough by hand, mix together the flour, salt, and aniseeds and stir them into the yeast mixture in 2 additions. Beat in the butter or lard 1 piece at a time and stir until well blended. Knead on a lightly floured work surface for 7 to 10 minutes, or until stretchy and elastic.

If you are making the dough in a heavy-duty electric mixer, mix the flour, salt, and aniseeds into the yeast mixture with the paddle attachment. Stir in the butter or lard 2 pieces at a time. Change to the dough hook and knead for about 3 minutes, or until the dough is slightly sticky, elastic, and can be pulled up into peaks with your fingertips.

First rise. Place the dough in a lightly oiled container, cover tightly with plastic wrap, and let rise for 30 minutes.

Second rise. Divide the dough into 4 equal pieces and roll each into a ball. Place each one on parchment paper or on lightly floured rimless baking sheets or peels, cover with towels, and let rise for 1 hour. About 30 minutes before you plan to bake, preheat the oven to 425°F, with a baking stone inside, if you have one.

Shaping. Lightly oil two 10-inch metal pie pans or springform cake pans. Take 1 round of dough and flatten it so that it fills the bottom of the baking pan. Cover with a layer of grapes and sprinkle with about 1 tablespoon turbinado sugar. Flatten and stretch out a second ball of dough, place it on top of the grapes, and flatten it to cover the grape layer. Pinch the edges together very well. Cover with a second layer of grapes, press them lightly into the dough, and sprinkle 1 to 2 tablespoons of turbinado sugar over the top. Repeat with the remaining dough and grapes.

Baking. Place the baking pans in the oven on the baking stone and bake for 15 minutes. Reduce the temperature to 375°F, tilt the pan to collect the sugary syrup, and spread it along with a bit of Sambuca liqueur over the top of the dough. Continue baking until the top is golden brown, 15 to 20 minutes. Let cool for a few minutes in the pans, then slide the *schiacciate* out and let cool on a rack.

Makes two 10-inch schiacciate; serves 10 to 12
VARIATION: Use fennel seeds instead of aniseeds.
SCHIACCIATA BURSTING WITH RAISINS (*SCHIACCIATA ALL'UVA PASSA*): Use 3 cups raisins instead of grapes. Soak them in Vin Santo or another sweet wine and use the same wine in the dough.

Raisin-studded Cornmeal Focaccia
MAROKKA DOLCE

❀

Ligurians use the expression, "Rustica come la marokka," when they want to explain that something is a little rough, like the texture of this focaccia which is lightly crunchy with corn flour. A marokka is traditionally made with medium or coarse corn flour, which may be hard to find, but you can re-create the texture by blending flour and cornmeal in a food processor or blender.

⅓ cup dark raisins
2½ teaspoons (1 package) active dry yeast
1 cup water minus 1 tablespoon warm water, 105° to 115°F
3 tablespoons extra-virgin olive oil, preferably from Liguria
1¾ cups plus 1 teaspoon (250 grams) unbleached all-purpose flour
¾ cup (100 grams) cornmeal
1 teaspoon sea salt
Olive oil for brushing the dough

❧ Cover the raisins with warm tap water and let them plump for 30 minutes. Drain and pat them dry. Meanwhile, sprinkle the yeast over the warm water in a large mixing or mixer bowl; whisk it in and let stand until creamy, about 10 minutes. Stir in the olive oil. Blend the flour and cornmeal by whirling them in a food processor or blender for 30 to 45 seconds. If you are making the dough by hand, stir in the salt and the flour mixture in 3 additions, and mix with a wooden spoon until well combined. Knead by hand on a lightly floured work surface until the dough is elastic but still slightly sticky, 6 to 8 minutes.

❧ If you are making the dough in the heavy-duty electric mixer, use the paddle attachment to stir the combined flour and cornmeal with the salt into the yeast mixture. Mix at low speed until the dough is well combined. Change to the dough hook and mix for 3 minutes on low speed until the dough is elastic but still slightly sticky.

❧ First rise. Place the dough in an oiled container, cover it tightly with plastic wrap, and let rise until doubled, about 30 minutes. When ready, the dough will feel very delicate.

❧ Shaping and second rise. Turn the dough out onto a lightly floured work surface. Sprinkle the raisins over the surface, leaving a 1-inch margin all around. Fold in all 4 sides and roll the dough into a ball. Place in an oiled 8-inch pie pan, cover, and let rise until well risen, with obvious stretch marks in the dough, about 45 minutes.

❧ Baking. At least 30 minutes before you plan to bake, preheat the oven to 400°F with a baking stone inside, if you have one. Place the pan directly on the stone and bake for 5 minutes, then brush the top with olive oil and continue baking until the *marokka* is golden brown on top and underneath (check by lifting gently with a spatula), about 25 minutes. Let cool on a rack. Serve warm or at room temperature.

❧ *Makes one 8-inch focaccia; serves 6 to 8*

VARIATION: Use a heaping tablespoon of aniseeds in place of the raisins.

SAVORY MAROKKA (*MAROKKA SALATA*): Drain and pit ⅓ cup small black or green olives in brine and use them in place of the raisins.

Source List
FLOUR, INGREDIENTS, AND EQUIPMENT

American White Wheat Producers
P.O. Box 326
511 Commercial
Atchison, KA 66002
(913) 367-4422
Toll-free: (800) 372-4422
Fax #: (913) 367-4443
www.awwpa.com/
A source of white wheat flour

Arrowhead Mills
P.O. Box 2059
Hereford, TX 79045
(806) 364-0730
www.arrowheadmills.com
An excellent selection of stone-ground flours, including durum, corn flour, organic stone-ground whole wheat, and unbleached all-purpose white.

The Baker's Catalogue
P.O. Box 876
Norwich, VT 05055
Toll-free: (800) 827-6836
Fax #: (800) 343-3002
www.kingarthurflour.com
One-stop shopping for an extensive selection of flours and grains, as well as other baking ingredients and equipment. This is one of the few places to find white wheat flour.

The Chef's Catalogue
3915 Commercial Avenue
Northbrook, IL 60062
(312) 480-9400
Toll-free: (800) 338-3232
A source of Kitchen Aid mixers, baking stones, pizza peels, and scales.

Dean & DeLuca
Attn: Customer Assistance
2526 East 36th Street North Circle
Wichita, KS 67219
Toll-free: (877) 826-9246
Fax #: (800) 781-4050
www.deandeluca.com
An excellent selection of Italian products, including herbs, spices, olive oils, olives and olive paste, and grains and flours. Elderflower Concentrate also is available here.

Giusto's Speciality Foods Inc
344 Littlefield Avenue
South San Francisco, CA 94080
Toll-free: (888) 873-6566
Fax #: (650) 873-2826
www.giustos.com
Excellent organically grown stone-ground flours, as well as corn flour and cornmeal, yeast, and turbinado sugar.

Purity Foods, Inc.
2871 W. Jolly Road
Okemos, MI 48864
(517) 351-9231
Fax #: (517) 351-9391
www.purityfoods.com
The major source of spelt fours in this country; their products are carried in numerous natural foods stores.

Sassafras Enterprises, Inc.
1622 West Carroll Avenue
Chicago, IL 60612
(312) 226-2000
Fax #: (312) 226-0873
www.sassafrasenterprises.com
A superior source of baking stones, pizza peels, and pizza pans.

Sur la Table
Toll-free: (800) 243-0852
www.surlatable.com
A huge selection of kitchenware and equipment, including an oven insert that converts a gas or electric oven into a traditional brick oven for baking.

Todaro Bros.
555 Second Avenue
New York, NY 10016
Toll-free: (877) 472-2767
www.todarobros-specialty-foods.com
A huge selection of Italian ingredients, including olives, oils, and cheeses.

Williams-Sonoma
Toll-free: (877) 812-6235
Fax #: (702) 363-2541
A large selection of Italian ingredients including sun-dried tomatoes and olive oils. Plus electric mixers, instant thermometers, baking stones, scales, baking pans, and many other pieces of equipment.

Bibliography

Alberini, Massimo. *Liguri a Tavola*. Milano: Longanesi & C., 1965.

del Conte, Anna. *Gastronomy of Italy*. New York: Prentice Hall Press, 1987.

Genders, Ray. *Edible Wild Plants*. New York: van der Marck, 1988.

Innes, Jocasta. *The Country Kitchen Cookbook*. New York: Exeter Books, 1979.

Lingua, Paolo. *La Cucina dei Genovesi*. Padua: Franco Muzzio editore, 1989.

Marchese, Salvatore. *La Cucina di Lunigiana*. Padua: Franco Muzzio Editore, 1989.

———. *La Cucina Ligure di Levante*. Padua: Franco Muzzio Editore, 1990.

Nabhan, Gary Paul. *Songbirds, Truffles, and Wolves*. New York: Pantheon Books, 1993.

Ortiz, Elizabeth Lambert. *The Encyclopedia of Herbs, Spices, and Flavorings: A Cook's Compendium*. London: Dorling Kindersley, 1992.

Paracucchi, Angelo. *La Cucina della Lunigiana*. Milan: Longanesi & C., 1980.

Ratto, Giovanni Battista e Giovanni. *La Cuciniera genovese*. Genova: 1963.

Romer, Elizabeth. *Italian Pizza and Hearth Breads*. New York: Clarkson Potter, 1987.

Sada, Luigi. *Cucina pugliese alla poverella*. Foggia: I Quaderni del Rosone 7, 1991.

———. *La Gioia della Mensa*. Carbonara di Bari: Bibliotechina, 1980.

———. *La Cucina della terra di Bari*. Padua: Franco Muzzio Editore, 1991.

Willinger, Faith Heller. *Eating in Italy*. New York: Hearst Books, 1989.

Table of Equivalents

❀

THE EXACT EQUIVALENTS IN THE FOLLOWING TABLES
HAVE BEEN ROUNDED FOR CONVENIENCE.

METRIC

g – gram
kg = kilogram
mm = millimeter
cm = centimeter
ml = milliliter
l = liter

US/UK

oz = ounce
lb = pound
in = inch
ft = foot
tbl = tablespoon
fl oz = fluid ounce
qt = quart

OVEN TEMPERATURES

Fahrenheit	Celsius	Gas
250	120	½
275	140	1
300	150	2
325	160	3
350	180	4
375	190	5
400	200	6
425	220	7
450	230	8
475	240	9
500	260	10

LIQUIDS

US	Metric	UK
2 tbl	30 ml	1 fl oz
¼ cup	60 ml	2 fl oz
⅓ cup	80 ml	3 fl oz
½ cup	125 ml	4 fl oz
⅔ cup	160 ml	5 fl oz
¾ cup	180 ml	6 fl oz
1 cup	250 ml	8 fl oz
1½ cups	375 ml	12 fl oz
2 cups	500 ml	16 fl oz
4 cups/1 qt	1 l	32 fl oz

WEIGHTS

US/UK	Metric
1 oz	28 g
2 oz	56 g
3 oz	84 g
4 oz (¼ lb)	112 g
5 oz (⅓ lb)	140 g
6 oz	168 g
7 oz	196 g
8 oz (½ lb)	224 g
10 oz	280 g
12 oz (¾ lb)	296 g
14 oz	392 g
16 oz (1 lb)	450 g
1½ lb	675 g
2 lb	900 g
3 lb	1350 g

LENGTH MEASURES

US/UK	Metric
⅛ in	3 mm
¼ in	6 mm
½ in	12 mm
1 in	2.5 cm
2 in	5 cm
3 in	7.5 cm
4 in	10 cm
5 in	13 cm
6 in	15 cm
7 in	18 cm
8 in	20 cm
9 in	23 cm
10 in	25 cm
11 in	28 cm
12 in/1 ft	30 cm

Index

❦

Colophon

❀

This book is set in two families of typefaces. Deepdene, designed in 1927 by Frederick Goudy, was named for his house at Marlboro-on-Hudson, New York. The main text of the book is set in Fairfield, designed by Rudolph Rudzika, circa 1946.

❀

Book and cover design by Aufuldish & Warinner

❀

Photography by Joyce Oudkerk Pool
Food styling by Daniel Bowe
Joyce Oudkerk Pool and Daniel Bowe would like to thank the following people for all their help, support, kindness, and props.
Biordi, San Francisco; Viansa Winery, Sebastiani family, Sonoma; Zuni Cafe, San Francisco; Jan Stein, props; Gibson Scheid, props; Patricia Hart, props; Tim and Dean, props; Robert Sohigian, photo assistant; Virginia Morgan, assistant food stylist

❀